Introduction

Look around you. Your home or classroom is full of familiar, everyday objects. Calculators and compact discs, televisions and telephones, ballpoint pens and paperclips: nowadays, we take all these things for granted. But little more than a hundred years ago, none of these items had yet been invented.

This book brings together one hundred of these inventions. They have been chosen because most of them are things that we use or see every day. Many are used in the home, some in the workplace; some keep us entertained, others help us travel around. But they all have one thing in common: it is difficult to imagine life without them.

What makes people invent things? Sometimes it is the sheer adventure of it all. The pioneers of flight had little idea how useful aeroplanes would be. They just wanted to fly through the air like birds. Sometimes it is the answer to a pressing human need. Napoleon's need to feed his army on campaign led to the invention of canned food. Occasionally, inventions occur by accident. The inventor of the microwave oven had little interest in cooking at all. He was working for a radar equipment company when he discovered that microwaves could be used to produce heat.

But more often than not, people invent things because the existing technology does not seem to work well enough. Many of the inventions in this book were replacements for earlier, less effective inventions. The plough replaced the primitive digging stick. The paperclip replaced the pin as a way of holding papers together. Electric lights replaced oil and gas lamps. The sailing ship replaced the ship driven by oars, and was in turn replaced by the steamship. Even inventions like the telephone, which has no obvious ancestor, helped to replace the earlier telegraph system.

All of these inventions were great leaps forward. From time to time the leap would be made by a single inventor, working on his or her own. But more often, an invention is the product of a number of minds, either working together or independently, to try to make things better and make life easier for us all.

From the introduction of paper money and the earliest maps to the development of transistors; irons and the diesel engine – inventions through the ages have affected all aspects of our lives.

Weaving

The first clothes were made from animal skins, but it was not always easy to find enough skins to go round. It was a great day when someone invented the first loom, allowing people to weave cloth from thread that they had spun from the fleeces of sheep or goats.

Weaving goes back thousands of years, probably to at least 5000 BC. The first looms were 'ground looms'. These were made by pegging two parallel bars of wood to the ground and stretching a series of threads, the 'warp' threads, between them. The other thread, called the 'weft', was woven across and between the warp threads. Another early type of loom was called the 'backstrap loom'. In this type, the warp threads were attached to two horizontal bars.

▲ This clothworker holds a wooden shuttle, to which the weft thread is attached, in his right hand. He separates the warp threads with his left hand before passing the shuttle between them.

▼ On this nineteenth-century loom, a foot-pedal mechanism is used to hold the sets of warp threads apart while the shuttle is passed between them. The finished cloth is rolled up at the back of the loom.

People probably wove baskets out of straw before they realized how to use this technique to make textiles.

Sails

The first boats were simple dugout canoes or craft made of skin stretched over a wooden frame. They were propelled with paddles or oars. But sailing boats have a big advantage, because much bigger vessels can be powered without rowing.

No one knows for sure where or when the first sailing boats appeared. The way the wind pushes a boat along was probably discovered when someone held a large piece of cloth up in a boat. This may have happened on the Nile in Egypt, where there is a strong prevailing wind. The first known picture of a boat with a sail, dating from about 5,000 years ago, comes from the Nile valley. Areas such as Iran and Iraq, which have similar conditions, may also have seen early sailing boats. By the time of the pharaohs in Egypt, after about 3000 BC, sailing boats were common. There were many simple travelling and fishing boats that plied the Nile. They had a single square sail and a large oar aft (at the rear) used for steering. Masts made of wood and simple rigging to adjust the sail and point it in the right direction were also developed at this time.

We know that sailing vessels were well known by 3000 BC in Egypt, because pots decorated with pictures of sailing boats have survived from this time.

▼ Sailing boats still take advantage of the strong winds along the Nile. Today they usually have wedge-shaped sails like this vessel.

Saw

The people of the Stone Age could cut a variety of substances with their flint knives and axes. But very early on, they discovered that they could cut through tough materials more easily with a toothed or serrated edge. Archaeologists have discovered flint blades with serrated edges at least 10,000 years old.

But these serrated knives would not cut through wood. For that, a thin, sharp, metal saw was needed. No one knows for sure when such saws first appeared, but the ancient Egyptians probably had them before any other people, perhaps as early as 4000 BC. These saws had long, slim, sword-like blades attached to wooden handles. On the earliest saws, the cut was made on the pulling stroke, not on the pushing stroke as with most modern saws.

The Greeks and Romans inherited the sword-like saw of the Egyptians. The Romans also developed the 'frame-saw', a long metal blade mounted in a three-sided wooden handle. Saws like this were used for rough work. A frame-saw could be made large, and was often operated by two men, one standing on either side of the timber. Frame-saws are still widely used for cutting up logs and for work in timber yards. The modern version of the Egyptian saw is still used by carpenters for finer work.

▲ The ancient Egyptians were skilled wood-workers, using wood for everything from boats to furniture. This Egyptian relief shows a worker sawing wood for a boat from the Fifth Dynasty (2560–2460 BC).

Nowadays, many different types of saw are made for different tasks. The major difference is the size and frequency of the teeth. A small number of large teeth is adequate for rough work, while finer teeth make a smoother, neater cut.

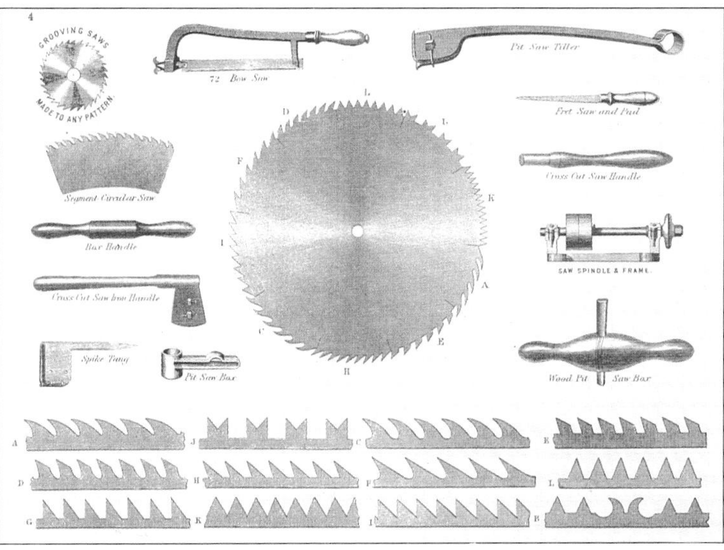

▶ A page from a nineteenth-century catalogue shows the range of saws available for different jobs. A variety of different tooth patterns allows for every type of sawing from fast, coarse cutting to slower, finer work. Thin saws like the pad saw (upper right) were for cutting intricate shapes like keyholes.

Lock

The idea of the lock probably appeared independently in different parts of the world. The ancient Chinese had simple locks that could be undone with a sickle-shaped or hook-like key. Locks like this existed in China at least 4,000 years ago, and probably earlier.

The people of ancient Egypt also protected their possessions with locks during the same period. These were slightly more sophisticated than the Chinese locks. Egyptian locks contained a series of pins of different lengths that corresponded to pegs that stuck out of the side of the key. Only a key with pegs of the right length would fit a particular lock. Unlike modern locks, which are made of hard metal, Egyptian locks were made of wood.

The Romans took over the idea of the lock from the Egyptians. They introduced new features, such as springs to press the pins down. The Romans took these locks with them when they conquered large parts of Europe, western Asia and northern Africa.

In the Middle Ages locks became very complex. Huge mechanisms of cogs, levers and springs were common in the lids of the chests and strongboxes where merchants and churchmen kept their valuables.

The modern Yale lock, invented by Linus Yale in the 1860s and still used widely, is based on the pin mechanism of ancient Egyptian locks.

◀ By the Roman period, locks and keys were quite common for securing houses and shops, as well as wooden chests containing valuables. This bronze lock-plate is Roman and comes from France. It was held in place by huge, heavy-headed nails.

Wheel

Nowadays wheels are everywhere, on cars, trains and aeroplanes, and in every kind of machine. It is hard to imagine a world without the wheel, a world in which heavy loads had to be dragged along the ground on sledges or rollers, and in which long-distance land transport was almost unheard of.

The wheel was first invented about 3500 BC in Mesopotamia, the land between the rivers Tigris and Euphrates in what is now Iraq. Wheels were first used on carts to transport heavy loads, and on chariots, which became favoured vehicles of war for peoples such as the ancient Egyptians and the Hittites (from modern Turkey).

To begin with, the usual way of making a wheel was to join three pieces of wood together with cross-planks. This created a square board that was cut to make a circle. In some places, where good wood was scarce, people even tried making wheels out of stone. These early wood or stone wheels were strong but heavy. They required a lot of pulling, so wore out their bearing fairly quickly.

Various attempts were made to make wheels lighter by cutting holes in the board, but the most effective was the spoked wheel, which was invented independently in northern Europe, China and western Asia, and was widespread after 2000 BC. By this time, wheels were common in many places, although some later civilizations, such as the Aztecs from central America, managed without wheels.

Chinese wheelwrights introduced a wheel with a slightly conical cross-section. This was more rigid than ordinary wheels, so a stronger wheel could be made with less timber, giving a useful saving in weight.

▼ Archaeologists unearthed this inlaid wooden box at Ur in Mesopotamia. The solid wooden wheels of the chariots can be clearly seen.

Potter's wheel

Pottery is one of the greatest inventions. It allows people to make long-lasting containers in a variety of shapes out of clay, which is available everywhere. The oldest pots that have been discovered were made in about 10,000 BC in Japan.

The earliest pots were made in one of two ways. Some were made by sticking the thumbs into a lump of clay to make a hole, then gradually pulling up the clay around the hole to form a vessel. Alternatively, a long 'sausage' of clay was coiled around in a spiral, so that the sides of a vessel were steadily built up. But it was hard to make the walls of the vessel the same thickness all the way around. An uneven or poorly balanced pot would be weak and easily broken.

In around 3250 BC in Mesopotamia, there was a breakthrough. Engineers were doing their first experiments with the wheel. Someone had the idea of mounting a wheel horizontally and 'throwing' a piece of clay on to it. Then, as the wheel was turned, the potter's fingers could shape the clay. Because the wheel was round, the pot would be symmetrical. And, with practice, it was easier to make sides of equal thickness.

▲ As his wheel spins, an Indian potter shapes a clay vessel with his fingers. A pot of water, to keep the clay and the potter's fingers moist, stands at the ready. The turning wheel makes it straightforward to make pots with quite complex shapes.

▼ The simple hand-turned wheel is still used in many parts of the world to make pots for everyday use. These were made in Agra, India, but similar ones are produced in many other countries.

Although potters' wheels are now usually turned by a motor instead of being pushed by the potter, they are essentially the same as those invented in Mesopotamia more than 5,000 years ago.

Glass

No one knows for sure when or where glass was first made. It probably appeared around 2600 BC in one of the early civilizations of Mesopotamia (modern Iraq) or Egypt.

Glass is made from a mixture of sand, limestone and sodium carbonate. Although we think of glass as a clear substance, ancient glass was not transparent. It was coloured because of the impurities in the ingredients, and these colours were often very beautiful.

The ancient Egyptians were superb glass artists, making small bottles and ornaments and often building up different colours in layers. Egyptian glass bottles from the Eighteenth Dynasty (1570–1320 BC) still survive.

Glass-blowing, or taking a blob of hot molten glass and blowing into it to make a hollow vessel, was a later invention. The first glass-blowers probably worked in Syria in the first century BC.

Glass windows were an even later invention. They too were originally made by blowing. A large vessel would be blown and then flattened to make a sheet of glass. Such glazed windows started to appear in around AD 100, but remained an expensive luxury for more than 1,000 years.

Old-fashion 'bull's-eye' windows, with a circular mark in the middle of the pane, were originally made from the bottom of a round blown vessel that had been flattened while still hot.

◀ This nineteenth-century engraving shows glass-blowers in Egypt. The men in the foreground are finishing off a large glass vessel; the worker on the left is beginning to blow a small blob of glass; and the man on the right is heating glass in a furnace.

Maps

The first maps were made by people in Mesopotamia (modern Iraq) in around 2250 BC. To begin with, maps covered only a small local area. They were usually used to show individual plots of land, or to indicate proposals for new buildings.

The ancient Egyptians also found maps useful to show property ownership. This was because they lived by the River Nile, which flooded each year. The flood waters moved the boundary stones, so a map could settle any disputes about ownership.

The ancient Greeks used maps in a more adventurous way. When they sailed around the Mediterranean founding new colonies, they included these on maps. They built up a picture of their world and made it easier for people to find their way around. They also drew world maps. Perhaps the greatest of these early geographers was Ptolemy (c. AD 100–165). He wrote a book, called *Geographia,* about map-making, describing different projections or ways of representing the Earth's curved surface on a flat surface.

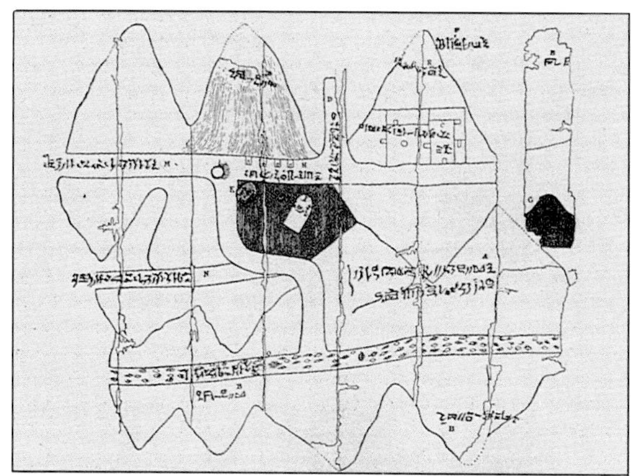

▲ This map comes from an ancient Egyptian papyrus. It shows local features such as irrigation canals, and indicates who owned the land.

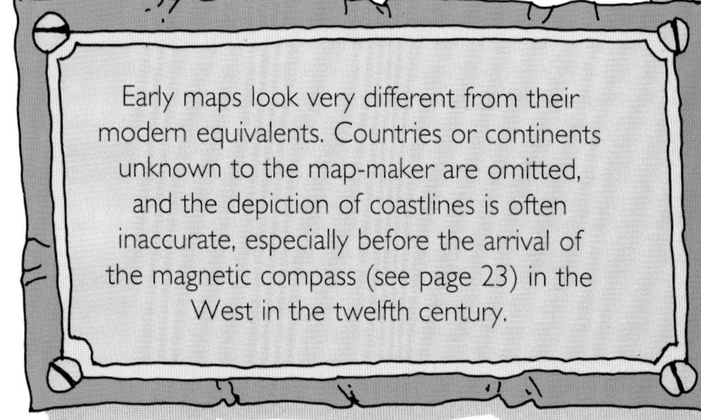

Early maps look very different from their modern equivalents. Countries or continents unknown to the map-maker are omitted, and the depiction of coastlines is often inaccurate, especially before the arrival of the magnetic compass (see page 23) in the West in the twelfth century.

▼ Ptolemy's map gives an accurate picture of the Mediterranean, but is less reliable for other areas.

Plough

The first farmers broke up the soil with a simple digging stick or hoe. Then, they threw their seed on the ground and hoped for the best. But around 5,500 years ago, farmers in Mesopotamia and Egypt began to try a new way of breaking up the soil: the plough. Early ploughs were made from a Y-shaped piece of wood. The lower branch was carved to a point, the upper branches made two handles. When ropes were attached and the plough was pulled by an ox, the point scratched a narrow, shallow furrow in the soil. The farmer could steer the plough with the handles.

In the dry, sandy soils of Egypt and western Asia, this early scratch plough broke up the dry ground well and crop yields were much improved. The increased food supply may well have led to a rise in population and the increasing success of the cities of Egypt and Mesopotamia. By 3000 BC, farmers were improving their ploughs by carving the point to make a sharp 'share' to cut the soil more effectively, and a flat, sloping 'sole' to push the soil aside.

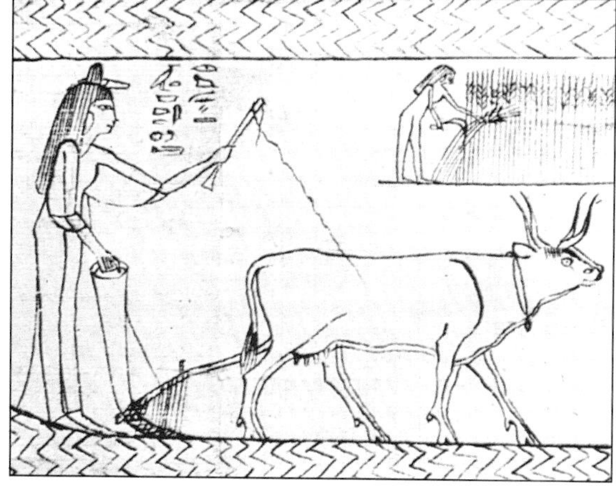

▲ In about 970 BC, this drawing of a simple wooden ox-drawn plough was made in Egypt. The design has changed little from the first ploughs which were made as long ago as 3500 BC.

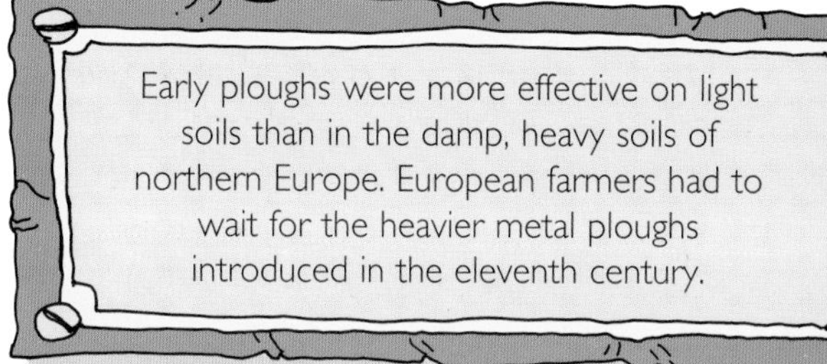

Early ploughs were more effective on light soils than in the damp, heavy soils of northern Europe. European farmers had to wait for the heavier metal ploughs introduced in the eleventh century.

▼ The wooden plough, pulled by oxen, is still used in many parts of the world, especially where the soils are light and sandy.

Alphabet

The first people to write were probably the ancient Mesopotamians, who lived in what is now Iraq. They were writing by the fourth millennium BC. But they did not use an alphabet. They used a script called 'cuneiform', which was written on clay tablets with a reed stylus. There was a separate sign for each word, so people had to learn thousands of symbols.

It was probably the Phoenicians who first had the idea of the alphabet. Their eastern Mediterranean civilization was at its peak in around 1600 BC. They had an empire based on sea trade, so writing was important to them for recording accounts and contracts.

The Phoenicians invented a system that had a separate symbol for each consonant sound. Words were written by spelling out the sounds. It was a brilliant idea because anyone who wanted to write only had to learn some twenty symbols. The Phoenician alphabet was so successful that later systems, such as the Greek alphabet and the Roman alphabet that is used in the West today, are derived from it.

▲ The ancient Egyptians wrote with symbols called hieroglyphs. The signs were often simplified pictures, such as a wavy line to represent water.

Whereas written Chinese uses a total of more than 50,000 different signs, the modern Roman alphabet has only twenty-six letters. Most Chinese people only learn a few thousand signs, but languages using the Roman alphabet are far easier to read and write.

▼ This clay tablet from the ancient city of Babylon is written in the wedge-shaped cuneiform script. A reed stylus was used to make the marks in damp clay, which was left in the sun to harden.

Iron working

Today, there is iron or steel almost everywhere you look. Cars, buildings and appliances in the home all contain large amounts of iron. It is a material that can be found in many places on the Earth's surface; it is easy to work and it is strong and durable, so long as it is not allowed to rust. But for thousands of years people did not know about iron. Since it is found in a rocky 'ore', its presence is not obvious. It was probably first discovered somewhere in western Asia, perhaps in Syria, or by the Hittite people of Turkey, around 2000 BC.

To make iron suitable for working, the ore bearing the metal has first to be heated and the molten metal collected. This is called 'smelting'. Molten iron can be poured into moulds to cast objects, but the resulting 'cast iron' is weak and brittle. So 'wrought iron' was developed by taking a piece of iron that had been smelted and hammering it repeatedly, to form the shape of the item they wanted to make. The hammering, as well as shaping the metal, gave it extra strength.

▲ These ironworkers are smelting iron ore using a blast furnace. The ore is added at the top and the molten metal is collected at the base.

▼ These metalworkers are heating iron in a forge. They will then use their tongs to take out the red-hot metal, which can then be beaten into shape.

Bronze (an alloy of copper) continued to be used for hundreds of years after the discovery of iron, even though iron is much more plentiful, because it took time for ironworkers to discover how to make iron harder and stronger by beating.

Dyes

Dyes have been used for thousands of years. Cave paintings from the Upper Palaeolithic period (35,000 to 10,000 years ago) show that people already knew how to reproduce colours. But whereas cave artists used mainly colours derived from the earth, people preferred dyes made from plants for their clothes.

The first dyes were probably made several thousand years ago. People discovered a number of plants that would give bright-coloured dyes when they were boiled in water. Woad gives blues and purples; saffron and safflower give yellows; madder, which has been grown for over 2,000 years, makes red.

Other sources of dye include the cochineal beetle, a type of insect that produces a red colouring. This is one of the most ancient dyes, and can still be used as food colouring. The Phoenicians, who lived in the eastern Mediterranean around 1500 BC, used a purple colour from molluscs called *Murex*. This costly dye was also prized by the Romans, who used it for their emperors' garments.

Compared with modern synthetic dyes, natural dyes have many problems. They are not permanent, and fade in the sun or run in the rain. Cloth-makers discovered that adding chemicals to the dye would make them longer lasting. These chemicals are known as 'mordants'.

▼ Natural dyes produce vivid colours and they are still used in many places, such as India. In the industrialized world, however, they have been replaced by synthetic dyes.

Thermometer

The Italian scientist Galileo (see pages 31 and 33) came very close to inventing the thermometer in 1592. He made an instrument called a 'thermoscope'. In it, an open-ended tube was held over a container of water. The level of water in the tube varied with the temperature in the room. But unfortunately, the level also changed when the air pressure varied.

Duke Ferdinand II of Tuscany was fascinated with Galileo's apparatus and experimented with it in the early seventeenth century. In 1644 he sealed the unit from the surrounding air, and thereby removed the influence of the air pressure.

But the first thermometer that resembled the ones we know today was the mercury thermometer. This was perfected by a Dutch instrument-maker, D. G. Fahrenheit, in the early eighteenth century.

This type of thermometer works because substances expand as they get hotter. The thermometer consists of a narrow glass tube with a bulb at the bottom.

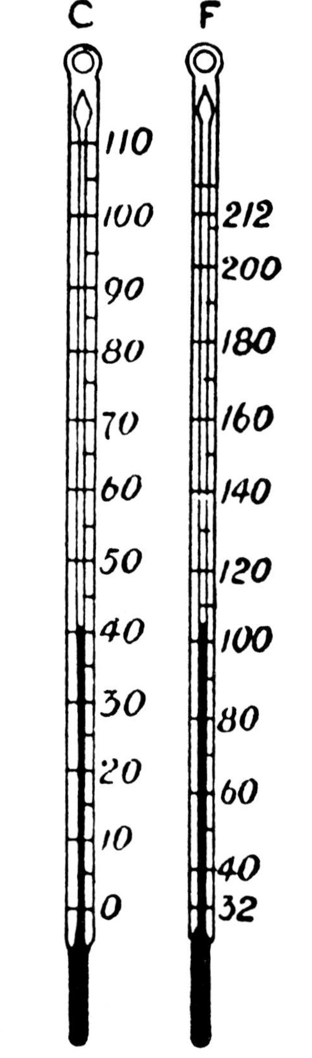

The first time a mercury thermometer was used by a physician to measure the temperature of the human body was in 1867 by Thomas Allbutt.

The bulb is filled with a liquid such as mercury. When the temperature goes up, the liquid expands and is forced up the tube. The temperature is read on a scale on or next to the tube.

Fahrenheit also introduced a scale of temperature measurement that was named after him. The Fahrenheit scale was widely used in the past, but today the Celsius or centigrade scale, developed by Swedish astronomer Anders Celsius in 1742, is preferred.

◀ This nineteenth-century engraving depicts the making of the first thermometers. The narrow glass tubes, with their bulbs for the mercury, are clearly visible.

Screw

Nowadays, nearly everything is fixed together with screws. Look around the home and you see screws holding together all sorts of items from furniture to food processors. The screw was invented more than 2,000 years ago, but has only been used for fixing for less than 500 years.

The first writer to describe a screw was the Greek scientist Archimedes (c. 287–212 BC). Archimedes' screw was a huge spiral enclosed in a wooden cylinder. It was used to raise water from one level to another to irrigate fields. Archimedes probably did not actually invent it himself. It is likely that he was just describing something that already existed. Ancient Egyptian engineers may have devised it for use in irrigation near the banks of the River Nile.

Archimedes' screw was used throughout the ancient world to raise water. But no one thought of adapting the idea as a fixing. During the Middle Ages, carpenters used wooden pegs or metal nails to hold together furniture and timber-framed buildings. During the sixteenth century, nail-makers started producing nails with a twist, which would hold more firmly. It was a short step from this type of nail to a screw. Screws became popular as fixings in the late eighteenth century, when a method was found of making them cheaply.

Screwdrivers appeared in London in around 1780. Carpenters found they could get a better fixing, and make better use of the fine screw threads being produced, by turning their screws with a screwdriver rather than hitting them with a hammer.

◀ Archimedes' screw was widely used for raising water. For example, the ancient Romans used it to get water out of mines.

Concrete

Concrete may seem like a very modern building material, but it was actually invented by the Romans. They made it by mixing fragments of stone with a mixture of lime and sand. The sand they used was volcanic earth called 'pozzuolana', which comes from the Pozzuoli region of Italy.

The Romans used concrete in many spectacular buildings. Structures like the Colosseum (shown below), the great amphitheatre in Rome, would have been very difficult to build without concrete.

After the fall of Rome in AD 476, something happened that is very unusual in the history of inventions. The art of making concrete with pozzuolana was forgotten in the West.

It was rediscovered in 1756 by British engineer John Smeaton, who was looking for a material with which to build the foundations of the Eddystone Lighthouse in Devon. Later engineers discovered that other sands could be substituted for pozzuolana, and the use of concrete in building became widespread once more.

▲ Concrete is ideal for lighthouse building because it will set underwater. It is tough, and so will withstand the pounding it gets from the waves.

In the 1860s, Frenchman Joseph Monier had the idea of reinforcing concrete with iron rods. This paved the way for the large-scale use of concrete in modern skyscrapers and other big buildings.

Compass

It is amazing to think that the sailors of Europe had no compasses to help them find their way until the twelfth century AD. Before that time, travelling by sea must have been both very difficult and very dangerous.

The first people to use a compass for navigation were probably travellers in China. A Chinese book of the fourth century BC contains the first written mention of the compass. To begin with, compass needles were made of 'magnetite', or 'lodestone', a black, naturally magnetic form of iron oxide. The Chinese noticed that a piece of magnetite that was allowed to move freely would invariably point north-south. They referred to their compasses as 'south-pointers' and were sometimes made to look like people – see the picture to the right.

Later, Chinese navigators discovered how easy it was to magnetize a piece of iron by rubbing it on a length of magnetite. Soon, they were making compasses that consisted of a piece of iron mounted on a disc of wood that floated in a bowl of water.

The compass did not come to Europe until it was described by the English writer Alexander Neckham in 1187. His work was followed up in 1269 by a book on magnetism by French writer Pierre de Maricourt. By this time, the floating compass had largely been replaced by the type of compass that is still familiar today.

Owners of early iron-clad ships often had problems because the magnetic effect of the iron in the ship 'fooled' the compass needle. Compasses had to be shielded in unmagnetized iron to get around this difficulty.

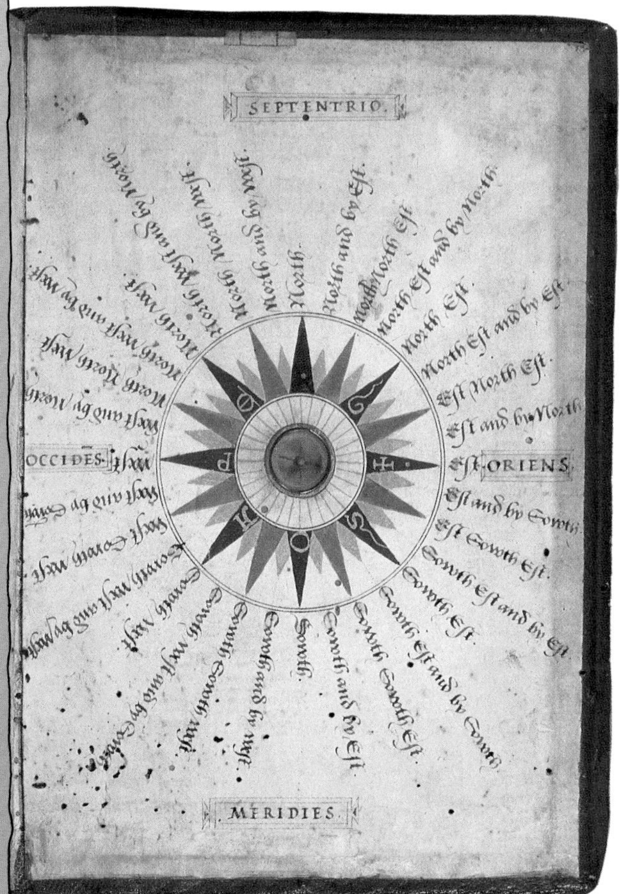

◀ This magnetic compass has been set into the cover of a set of sea charts that were used by navigators in the sixteenth century.

Paper

Ancient Chinese tradition gives us our first clue about the invention of paper. According to the chronicle of the Han Dynasty, an imperial official called Cai Lun invented paper in AD 105. Before this, the Chinese wrote on silk or slices of bamboo. In the West, people used parchment, made from animal hides.

No one knows for sure whether Cai Lun really invented paper, or whether he copied a manufacturing process that was already being used in rural China. But the emperor and his servant certainly knew what an important process it was.

The Chinese kept the art of paper-making a secret until about AD 800, when invading Muslims took some paper-makers prisoner.

The process that they guarded so carefully was fairly simple. A pulp was made of mulberry leaves beaten in a tub of water. Then, a thin layer of the pulp was lifted out of the tub on a tray.

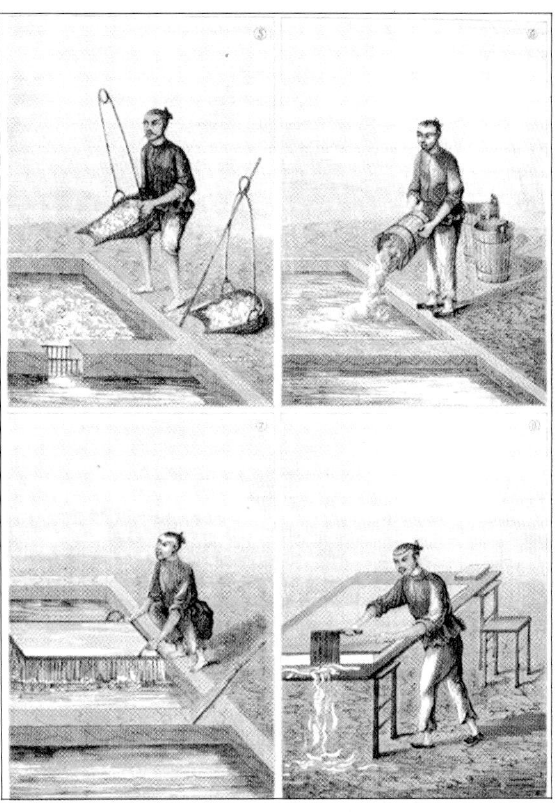

Today, paper is made in bulk, rather than in single sheets on the bamboo or metal trays of the early paper-makers. It is still made with pulp, although nowadays this often includes a high percentage of recycled paper.

This tray had a bamboo mesh in the base so that the water drained off, leaving a thin sheet of fibres. Finally, the sheets were squeezed to remove further moisture, and then dried.

The Europeans made paper in a similar way, but with linen rags or wood pulp instead of mulberry leaves. The European tray had a wire mesh rather than a bamboo base.

◀ These men are making paper the traditional way – placing layers of pulp on a tray between sheets of linen, and draining off the water.

Calendar

The calendar has been invented and reinvented many times and in many different places, as people noticed natural cycles such as the phases of the Moon and the passing of the seasons, and used these to measure time.

A society usually chose either a Moon-based 'lunar' calendar, or a Sun- and seasons-based 'solar' calendar. These two basic systems are incompatible, because the lunar month of about 29.5 days produces a year of 354 days, whereas the solar year works out at just over 365 days. Cultures with lunar calendars preferred to keep their year in step with the cycle of the seasons, so they usually had to include extra months or days occasionally, to make the two separate years match up. The ancient Babylonians, for example, worked out a lunar calendar. Their year was divided up into twelve lunar months of equal length. They added an extra month now and then, so that their lunar calendar also fitted in with the cycle of the seasons. By the fourth century BC, they had worked out how to do this in a systematic way. The ancient Egyptians used both lunar and solar calendars. The lunar calendar was used by the priests, the solar calendar by the farmers.

Today, most places use the Gregorian calendar, which was established in 1582. It is named after Pope Gregory XIII. Its twelve months started life as lunar months, but some have had extra days added to them, to make up a full solar year.

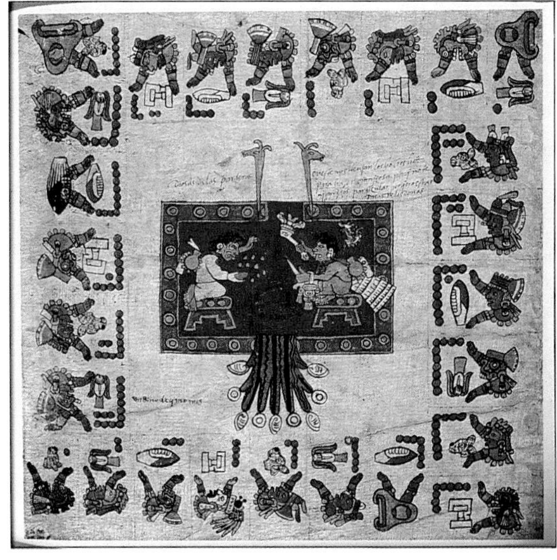

▲ This manuscript from Mexico shows the story of the invention of the Aztecs' calendar.

◀ Because of the link with the phases of the Moon, the signs of the zodiac always correlate with the Western calendar.

The days of the Gregorian months normally add up to 365. A full solar year is actually 365.2422 days long, which means that there is a need for one extra day every four years. This is why we add one day every fourth year, to make a leap year.

Windmill

The first windmills were built in western Asia, probably in Syria, in the seventh century AD. In this part of the world, there are strong winds that almost always blow in the same direction. So these early mills were built facing the prevailing wind. They did not look like the windmills seen today, but had upright shafts, with the sails arranged vertically, in an arrangement similar to the horses on a roundabout.

The first windmills appeared in western Europe at the end of the twelfth century. Some people think that soldiers returning home from the Crusades in Palestine brought back news of windmills. But Western mills are designed so differently from those in Syria that they may have been invented independently.

Western windmills look different because the sails move around in a vertical plane. Because winds are more variable in Europe than in western Asia, they also have a mechanism to turn the sails into the wind.

▲ Typical Mediterranean windmills have circular stone towers and vertical sails set towards the prevailing wind. They are still used for grinding corn.

Windmills are rarely used to grind grain today, but are enjoying a new lease of life as a way of generating electricity. 'Wind farms' consist of large groups of windmills driving generators.

▼ Modern windmills connected to generators provide electricity at Aero Island, St Rise, Denmark.

Clock

We take it for granted today that we can glance at a clock to tell the time. But for thousands of years, there was no accurate method of time measurement at all. People had to judge the time by the position of the Sun in the sky, or get along with devices like sundials or hourglasses in which the time was indicated by the falling of sand through a double-ended glass vessel.

The person to change this was a Chinese engineer called Xi Ying, who lived in the eighth century AD. Together with another Chinese inventor, Liang Lingzan, he devised the 'escapement', the arrangement of cogs at the heart of all mechanical clocks.

Mechanical clocks came to Europe in the Middle Ages. By the fourteenth century, large, unwieldy mechanical clocks were being built in Europe. They were driven by weights, and were only accurate to within about an hour per day. Clocks like this did not usually have faces. They were connected to a bell that struck the hours. Since they were so inaccurate there would have been little point in a mechanism that showed the minutes or seconds! Spring-driven clocks were developed in the fifteenth century. More accurate clocks with pendulums followed in the seventeenth century.

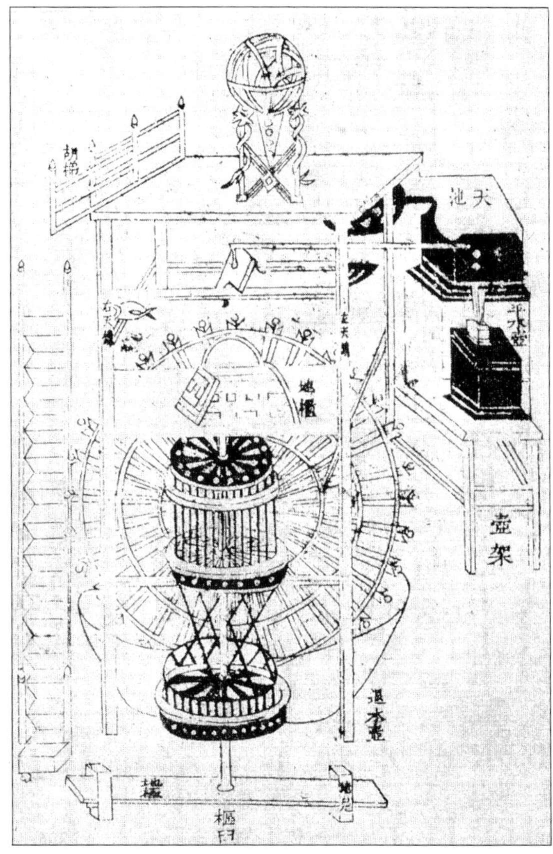

▲ Little is known about ancient Chinese clocks, but this one, built in the eleventh century by the astronomer Su Song, was powered by a waterwheel.

Medieval clock-makers built clocks that displayed the motion of the Sun and the phases of the Moon and the planets, as well as showing the time. Sometimes mechanical figures struck bells to sound out the hours and quarter hours.

◀ This page from an old catalogue shows the variety of clocks, both spring and pendulum driven, that were available by the nineteenth century.

Paper money

The first money was made of materials that were valuable in the place where the money was made. A golden guinea was made of an amount of gold that was actually worth that amount. Sometimes, these materials were rather cumbersome, for example heavy stones, shells and, most commonly, metal, were all used as money in different parts of the world.

In tenth-century China people were fed up with the heavy metal coins issued by the government. So some people started to deposit the coins with merchants, who would give them a receipt. The receipt was then passed from person to person in exchange for goods or services. In other words, it was used as money.

The Chinese government soon saw the advantages of this system. In the early eleventh century, they printed their own receipts and gave them standard values to make the system easier to use. They had made the first banknotes.

Printed money came to Europe in 1661, when Swedish bankers started to produce notes as a result of a silver shortage. In the USA, paper money appeared early. The colonists made their first paper dollars before they broke away from Britain in 1776. Paper currency became a powerful symbol of American independence.

The largest banknote ever produced was a Chinese note that measured 22.8 x 33 cm (9 x 13 ins). The equivalent Chinese coins of the time would have weighed around 8 lb (3.5 kg).

◀ During the 1920s in Germany, prices rose dramatically and the German currency, the Mark, became almost worthless. Banks had to issue notes worth millions of Marks, like this five million-Mark note of 1923.

Spectacles

The first person to have the idea of improving his sight with spectacles was a scientist from Florence, Salvino degli Armati. He used a pair of convex lenses to correct long sight in about 1280. He revealed the secret of his invention to a friar called Alessandro della Spina, who came from Pisa. Della Spina told others how to make spectacles, pointing out how the glass had to curve. By the fourteenth century, a number of people in Italy wore glasses. In the following century, concave lenses, suitable for correcting short sight, were produced.

Spectacles did not catch on quickly, mainly because the craft of lens grinding was not fully developed. For any lens to work well, the surface has to be smooth and the curve consistent. Lens-makers were still having trouble producing lenses of the right quality in the seventeenth century, when microscopes (see page 31) and telescopes (see page 33) were being developed. By this time, there was also a greater demand for glasses, partly because more people were learning to read than ever before, and so spectacle-wearing became more and more common.

▲ This wall painting from a church at Treviso, Italy, is the first picture of someone wearing spectacles. The picture was painted in 1362.

It was the American scientist and diplomat Benjamin Franklin who invented bifocals in 1780. Bifocals are spectacles with twin lenses that enable the wearer to see close objects when looking down, and distant scenes when looking up.

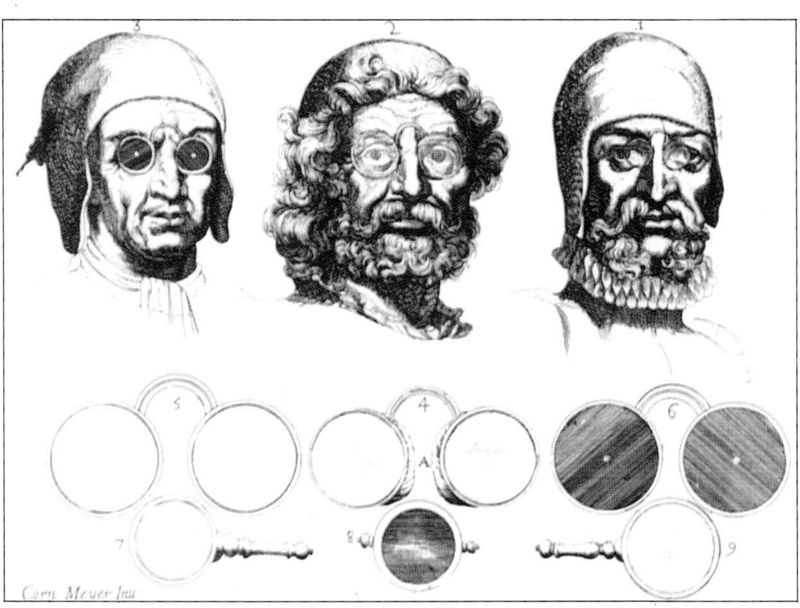

◀ The thick glass lenses of early spectacles were held in place by frames of wood or horn. For most people, there was one simple style of frame.

Spinning

Our early ancestors wore clothes made of animal skins. But at some point, several thousand years ago, people worked out how to spin thread to make textiles. It is impossible to know when or where this craft began, because it dates from the time before written records, and most ancient textiles have long since rotted away. In addition, the first thread was probably spun by hand, without any equipment, so no tools have survived either. So we must try to piece together the evidence we have.

The first thread was probably spun from the fleece of a sheep or goat. The natural fibres were taken from the animal, perhaps originally when the creature was moulting. The threads were disentangled and then drawn out to give a thread of the right thickness. Finally, the fibres were twisted to make them stronger. To begin with this was done by twisting the fibres between the palm of one hand and the thigh.

▲ This illustration is based on a fifth-century painting from ancient Greece. It shows that Greek women of this period still used the simple spindle. The thread they produced was woven into fine fabrics to make their beautiful pleated dresses.

The spinning wheel appeared during the Middle Ages, probably in Italy. The first spinning wheels were introduced into England during the fourteenth century.

Soon, people learned to use a 'spindle'. In its simplest form, this is a slender spinning tool that is spun by hand and allowed to fall, thereby drawing and twisting the fibres. Ancient spindles usually consisted of a thin stick weighted by a round stone called a 'whorl'.

◀ The spinning wheel keeps the spindle turning. In the simplest type, the operator pushes the wheel with one hand to turn the spindle, while pulling out the fibres to make a thread with the other hand. Here, the wheel is turned with a treadle.

Microscope

The microscope is one of the greatest inventions of all time. Before it was invented, our idea of the world around us was limited to what we could see with the naked eye, or the naked eye assisted by a simple hand lens. The microscope opened up a whole new world to our gaze. People saw for the first time hundreds of 'new' tiny creatures and plants, and the inner structure of everything from human tissue to plant fibres. Microscopes continue to help scientists discover new species and doctors cure diseases.

The first microscopes were made in Holland in the late sixteenth century. The inventor may have been a Dutch optician called Zacharias Jansen or another Dutch scientist, Hans Lippershey (see page 33). These men made simple microscopes with two lenses. They did not make any important observations through these instruments.

Later, two men started to use the microscope scientifically. The first was the Italian scientist Galileo (see page 33), who first described the complex eye of an insect after looking at it through a microscope. The second was the Dutch linen merchant Antonie van Leeuwenhoek (1632–1723), who taught himself to grind lenses. He described for the first time many microscopic plants and animals that are invisible to the naked eye.

▲ This microscope belonged to the seventeenth-century British scientist Robert Hooke. It has a simple leather tube containing the lenses, mounted on an adjustable stand. A glass globe filled with water is used to focus light on to the subject.

Ernst Ruska revolutionized biology in 1931 by developing the electron microscope. This allowed scientists to observe objects as small as one-millionth of a millimetre. He was awarded a Nobel Prize in 1986.

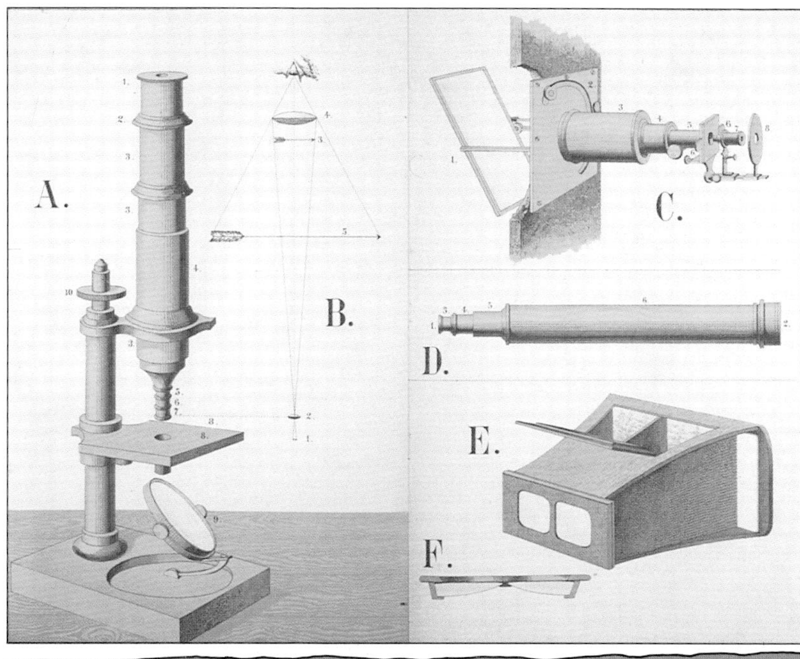

▶ The diagram shows a range of early optical instruments, and the paths of rays of light through a microscope.

Watch

Today, wrist-watches are cheap and keep good time. Nearly everyone wears one and can tell the time at a glance. But this has not always been so. The first clocks were so large that the idea of one you could wear on your wrist must have seemed absurd.

Early clocks were powered by moving weights, so they would not work when they were carried around. But in the fifteenth century, clock-makers learned to use a coiled spring to power a clock. This type of mechanism is not affected by movement in the same way as the weights of the early clocks.

In the early seventeenth century, the first watches, powered by coiled springs, were produced. But they were not very accurate. Watches were much improved by the appearance of the balance spring, invented by Dutchman Christiaan Huygens in 1675. This regulated the watch, making it keep much better time.

Nowadays, most people have a quartz watch. This contains a tiny crystal of quartz, which vibrates at a set frequency. The watch movement converts the vibrations of the quartz into the motion of the hands.

All these early watches looked like miniature clocks and were designed to be carried in the pocket. Wrist-watches only appeared as a fashion accessory in the 1880s. But in the twentieth century, wrist-watches caught on. Now most people wear one, so that they can see the time instantly, wherever they are.

◀ By the twentieth century, both pocket and wrist-watches were available, and people took it for granted that they would always be able to tell the time. Watches ranged from jewelled luxury items to cheap models with simple faces.

Telescope

Lenses had been around for hundreds of years before someone thought of putting two of them together to obtain a magnified image. No one knows for sure who first did this, but it was probably a Dutch spectacle-maker of the early seventeenth century. The first person to patent a telescope was the Dutch optician Hans Lippershey (see page 31), who applied for his patent in 1608.

Lippershey started making telescopes straight away. He sold a number to the Dutch government. They were probably wanted for military or marine use, as sailors soon realized that a telescope was invaluable on board ship.

The Italian scientist Galileo (see also pages 20 and 33) heard about Lippershey's telescopes, and in 1609, made one for himself. He made improvements in design, and was soon studying the planets and stars.

A later scientist who improved the telescope was Isaac Newton. Newton used spherical mirrors as well as lenses to produce 'reflecting' telescopes, finding that this was a way to cut out colour distortion.

Galileo made startling discoveries with his telescopes. He studied the Sun, Venus, the planet Jupiter and its moons, and many other heavenly bodies. His observations eventually led to a whole new view of the universe. Since Galileo's time, the telescope has been the most important instrument in astronomy.

◀ Modern telescopes like this one at an observatory in Nice, France, have huge lenses and mirrors, to look far into the night sky.

Submarine

There are many ancient tales of people travelling underwater in primitive submarines. The Macedonian leader Alexander the Great is said to have used a glass barrel to travel underwater. Stories like this are probably legends. But Dutchman Cornelius van Drebbel certainly did build a submarine in the seventeenth century. Powered by oars, he rowed it under the surface of the River Thames in London in 1615. The English king, James I, was impressed.

Another famous early submarine was the *Turtle*, built by American David Bushnell in 1775. It was driven by a screw propeller, which was powered by a handle turned by the driver.

The *Turtle* was used unsuccessfully to attack enemy ships in the American War of Independence (1775–83). But human-powered submarines were not very effective. Handles did not give enough power. The engineers of the nineteenth century also found it difficult to make seals for the propeller shafts and doors. It was not until efficient petrol engines were developed that submarines really came into their own.

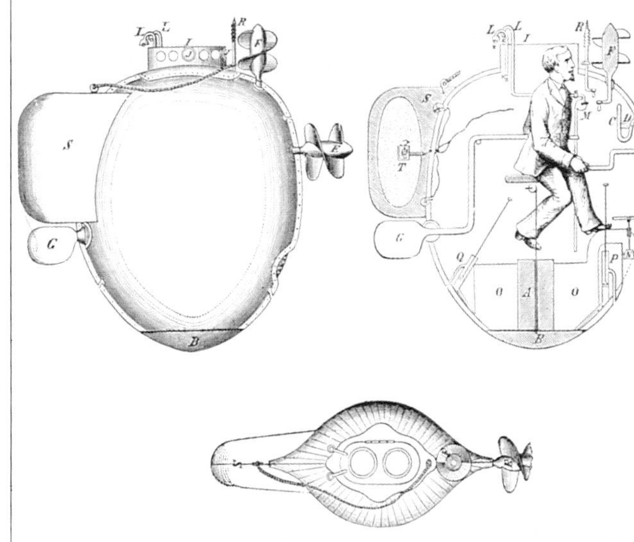

▲ The *Turtle* had two propellers, one (F) for vertical movement, the other (E) for movement in a horizontal line. There was a rudder (G) for steering.

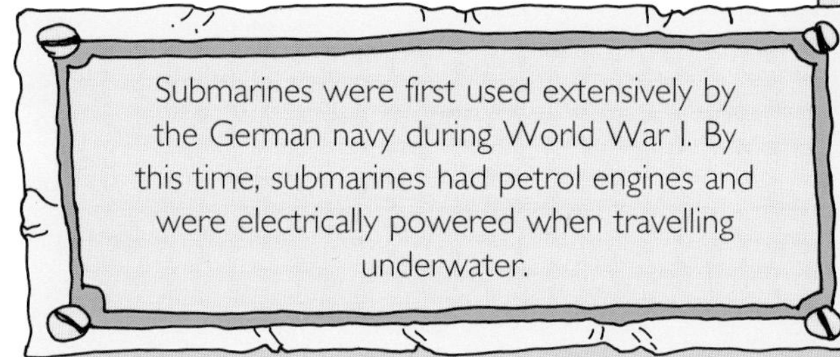

Submarines were first used extensively by the German navy during World War I. By this time, submarines had petrol engines and were electrically powered when travelling underwater.

▼ On a modern submarine there is an array of instruments to give the crew information on everything from the vessel's speed and depth to the pressure of the water outside.

Matches

Nowadays, fire can be made instantly, at the stroke of a match. But before the nineteenth century, it was much more difficult. People usually used a device called a 'tinder box'. This contained a flint, which was struck against a piece of the mineral iron pyrites, to make a spark. The spark set alight a piece of dry 'tinder', which was made of material such as wood shavings.

Around 1800, someone had the idea of replacing the tinder with a small splint of wood tipped with sulphur. Matches as we know them today were developed from these splints. A British chemist, John Walker, made the first matches that could be 'struck' in 1826. He made a paste of sulphide of antimony and chloride of potash and smeared this on to a spill. In 1831, chemists began to use white phosphorus, a flammable but toxic chemical, in the tips of matches. In 1845, the chemist Anton von Schrötter discovered safer red phosphorus, which was used on matches after 1852.

Modern matches usually contain no phosphorus. The phosphorus is generally in the striking surface, while the match itself is tipped with chemicals that will burst readily into flame.

▼ John Walker's matches burst into flames when scraped along a piece of sandpaper. They were successful, even if they were not always easy to light. Walker called them 'Lucifers'.

Seed drill

When an early farmer wanted to sow some seed, he walked across the field throwing handfuls of seed on the ground as he went. This method, called 'broadcasting', was very unreliable. A lot of seed would land in some places, while other areas would receive very little.

The answer, of course, was to sow the seed in neat rows. But how could this be done? The people of ancient Mesopotamia invented the first seed drill, or machine for sowing seed, in around 3500 BC. It was a box with a narrow tube that could be carried along the straight furrows made by a plough.

But the first really efficient seed drill was not made until 1701, by the English farmer and inventor Jethro Tull. Tull saw that the problem with early seed drills was they did not deliver the seed evenly. The seed would be sown in a straight line, but there would often be gaps in the line. So Tull invented a spring mechanism that delivered the seed in an even, continuous stream.

With seed sown in this way, each plant stood a good chance of growing well and weeds were easier to remove with the wheat planted in lines. The result was better harvests, more profit for farmers, and a more reliable food supply.

▲ The traditional way to sow was to fill a bag with seed and scatter it by hand over the field.

Jethro Tull was a keen amateur musician and used his musical knowledge for his invention. He got the idea for the spring device in his seed drill from part of the sounding-board mechanism of the organ.

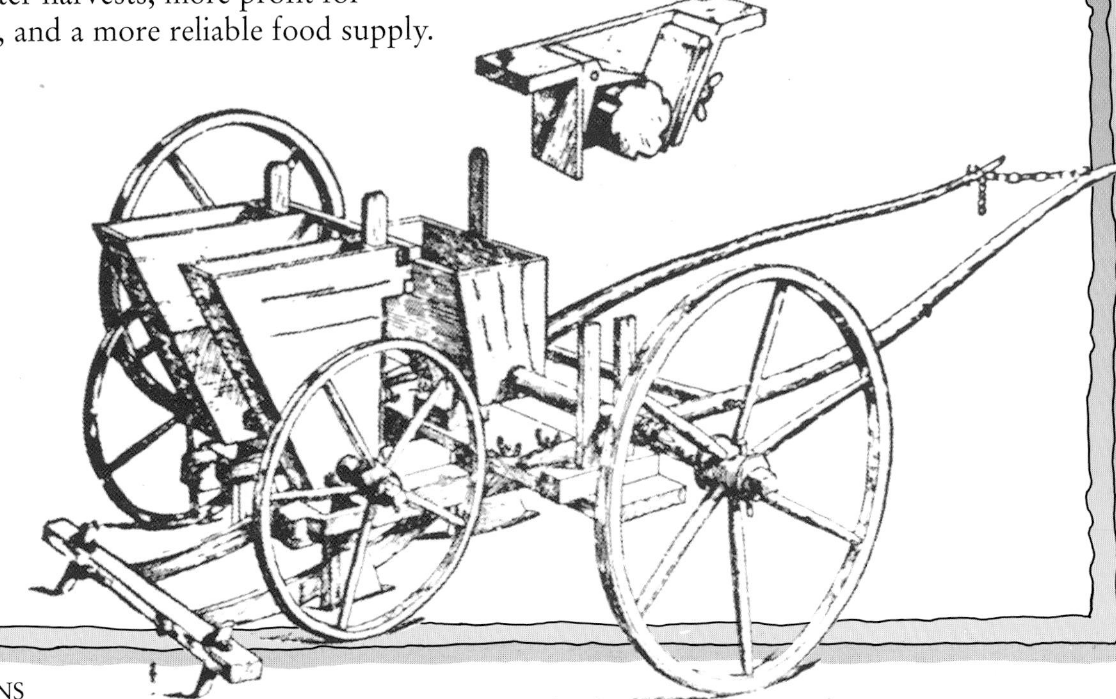

False teeth

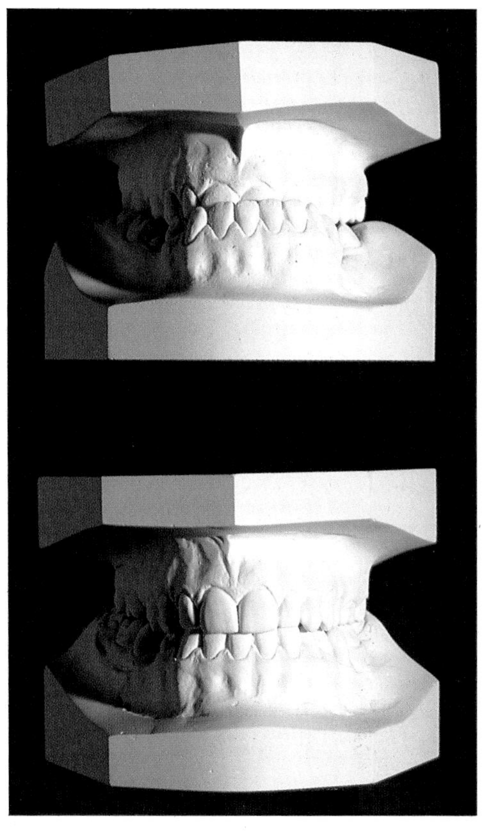

Tooth decay has always been a problem. The ancient Etruscans of northern Italy were making false teeth with gold by around 700 BC. But dental work of this quality was unusual until the eighteenth century. It was difficult to make teeth that fitted the patient properly and upper false teeth kept falling out. Sometimes wearing false teeth was almost as bad as the pain of tooth decay itself!

An eighteenth-century Parisian dentist called Fauchard was the first to make false teeth with steel springs, to keep the upper teeth in the top of the mouth. But even these rarely fitted well, and ivory, the traditional material for the teeth, decayed after a while and tasted unpleasant in the mouth. French dentists of the late eighteenth century introduced teeth of porcelain. The entire set of top or bottom teeth would be moulded in a single piece of porcelain. The result was a strong, long-lasting set of teeth, but they were still uncomfortable.

False teeth remained unpleasant to wear until the 1840s. Then, in 1844, American hardware merchant and inventor Charles Goodyear announced a new form of hardened rubber called vulcanite. When an impression of the patient's mouth had been made, the vulcanite could be moulded into a snugly fitting base for the false teeth. At last, it was possible to wear false teeth that were both comfortable and long-lasting.

To make well-fitting false teeth, the dentist has to make an accurate impression of the patient's mouth. The first person to do this was probably the Frenchman Dubois de Chemant, who used to pushed wax into his patients' mouths to make an impression.

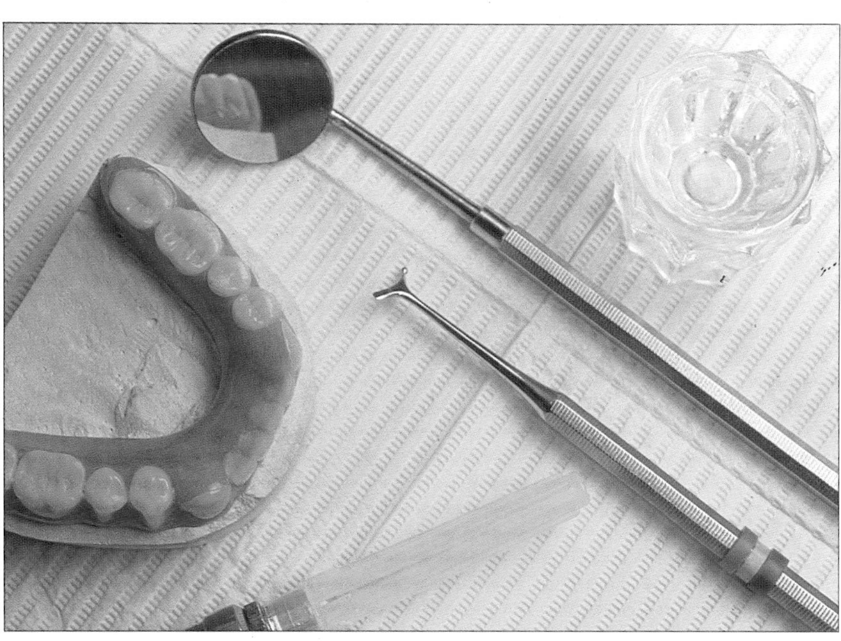

▶ Modern dental technicians can produce false teeth that look very much like the natural teeth they are designed to replace. These teeth also fit well and are comfortable to wear.

Steamship

▲ The early paddlesteamers were so successful that such vessels were soon carrying many passengers on short journeys along the rivers of North America.

Sailing ships could travel fast – so long as there was a wind. In the eighteenth century ship owners began to dream of vessels powered by steam. Such ships would be able to sail in all weathers.

In 1775 inventors started to design different ways of making the power of a steam engine drive a ship. To begin with, most people preferred paddle wheels, based on the design of the water wheel. But American inventor Benjamin Franklin suggested jet propulsion, in which water was sucked in at the front of the ship and was forced out at the back. Another pioneer was the American James Rumsey, who was working at the same time as Franklin. He designed a boat propelled by steam-driven oars.

The designs of Franklin and Rumsey were not successful, and most of the first steamships were paddle steamers. Early examples included the *Comet*, designed by Patrick Bell in Scotland in 1812, and the *North River* (*Clermont*), built by Robert Fulton in the USA in 1807.

Improvements in steam engines during the nineteenth century made steamships even more popular. Important developments included the compound engine, with an extra cylinder, and the triple expansion engine, with three cylinders. Each was more efficient than its predecessor.

▼ After the appearance of propeller-driven vessels, steamships became the most widespread large passenger craft, both on rivers and at sea.

Water closet

The English queen Elizabeth I complained about the stench of unemptied chamber pots in her palace at Richmond. Her courtier Sir John Harington came to the rescue in 1595. When travelling in Italy, he had heard of an intriguing invention: a lavatory in which the waste was flushed away by water. One of Harington's water closets was installed at Richmond Palace.

Harington was so pleased with the idea that he published a book about it. But the water closet was not practical for most people when there were no mains drains to take the waste away, no running water and little money to pay for the plumbing. For most people, the chore of emptying chamber pots, or of letting the 'night soil man' take away the waste, continued.

A British inventor, Joseph Bramah, improved the design of the water closet in the late eighteenth century. Bramah introduced features such as the three-ball valve, which controls the flow of water filling the cistern, and the U-bend, which ensures that the smells of the waste pipe do not reach the user's nose. He patented his water closet in 1778.

Even a major city like London was not given mains drainage until the 1860s, when many people were able to take advantage of the WC for the first time. This was over 300 years after Harington's invention.

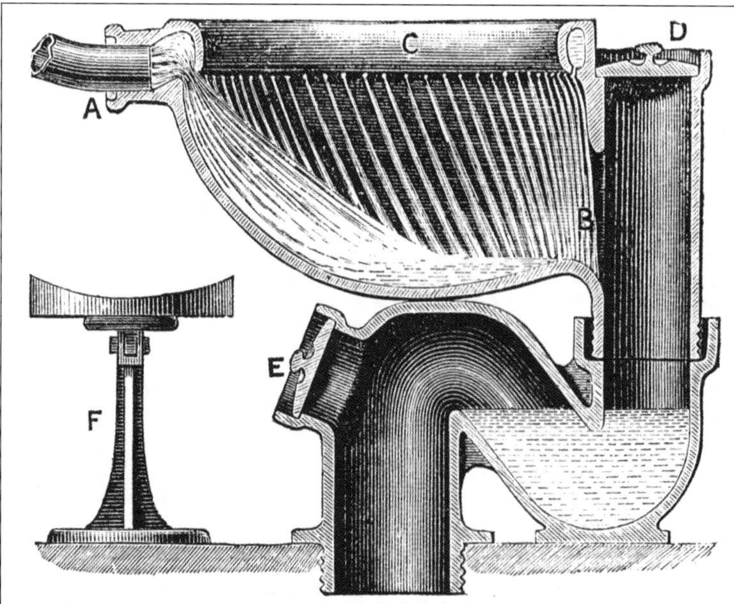

It was only in the late nineteenth century, when mains water and sewerage were installed in the towns and cities of Europe, that water closets could be used by the majority of people.

▼ One important feature of the water closet is the S-shaped pipe, or trap, which always holds some water. The water acts as a seal, keeping out smells.

Threshing machine

▲ These farm workers are winnowing, using a method that has not changed in some places for thousands of years. The wind blows away the chaff.

After wheat has been cut it has to be 'threshed'. This is the process that removes the grain from the husks and straw. The old way to do this was to beat the wheat with an instrument called a 'flail', which separated the husks and the grain. Then, the crop was 'winnowed', which entailed tossing it in the air so that the wind blew away the light, unwanted portions, the 'chaff', leaving just the grain behind. This was hard, back-breaking work, and it took a long time. The wheat from one acre (0.4 hectares) took about five days to thresh by hand.

Two men changed this, Scottish inventor James Meikle and his son Andrew. Working in the late eighteenth century, James developed a machine that contained a wooden frame that turned on a roller. Strips of leather were attached to the frame, and when it turned, a draught was created. This wind blew the husks away from the wheat. Andrew added a beating mechanism to the machine to loosen the husks.

The Meikle threshing machine could be driven by any power source to hand. They chose horses to drive the first machine, but soon water- and steam-powered versions had been made. The machines were very successful in the USA, where labour was in short supply and agriculture was on a large scale.

The threshing machine got a poor reception in Britain. Hand threshing gave farm workers winter employment. The threshing machine threatened to put many of them out of a job.

Batteries

Nowadays, we think of electricity as something that comes to us through a socket in the wall. But in 1800, there was no mains electricity, and the first electrical experiments were with the current produced by a battery.

It was the Italian physicist Alessandro Volta who produced the first battery. His countryman, biologist Luigi Galvani, had noticed something odd when dissecting a frog. When he touched the dead animal's legs with certain metals, they twitched. Volta thought that the twitching was the result of an electrical current that was produced by the metals. He began to experiment at the end of the eighteenth century. He found that he could produce an electric current by causing a chemical reaction between two pieces of metal, called 'electrodes', and certain solutions. He put these components together to make the first battery.

▲ Volta's 'pile' was a series of metal discs separated by moistened cloth pads.

Volta called his battery a 'pile', because it was a pile of zinc and copper discs separated by pads moistened with a weak solution of salt or acid. When a wire connected the top and bottom discs, a current flowed through the wire. The frog's body in Volta's earlier experiments had acted like the moistened cloth pads, and allowed a current to flow.

Volta's work was of great importance to modern physics. From it came all later developments in electricity, from electric motors to generators.

Later scientists honoured Volta by giving his name to one of the standard electrical units, the unit of electrical potential, or 'Volt'.

◀ Volta demonstrated his new battery or 'pile' to many scientists, including this French group. He had produced the first artificial source of electrical power – there were batteries long before electricity was available 'on the mains'.

Canned food

▲ Early canned food, like this can of sausages, was expensive, because the containers were filled and sealed by hand. Prices came down when machines were used in the canneries.

In the 1790s, the armies of Napoleon Bonaparte were marching across Europe. It was often difficult for them to get food, and in 1795, Napoleon offered a prize of 12,000 francs for a method of preserving food. A Paris confectioner and baker called Nicolas Appert read about the prize. Scientists at this time knew nothing about why food decayed, so he had to work by trial and error. After fourteen years of work, Appert made an important discovery. Liquid foods, like stews, and small fruit, such as raspberries, were preserved if he sealed them inside wine bottles and heated the bottles in boiling water.

The French army and navy tried out Appert's preserved foods and liked them. Appert was given the prize, together with a large contract to supply the French forces with bottled soup and vegetables.

A London merchant, Peter Durand, read about Appert's work. He had the idea of sealing the food in a metal can instead of using the breakable bottles. Durand did not develop the idea, though. He sold his patent to two British inventors, John Hall and Bryan Donkin. They used cans of steel covered with a thin layer of tin, sealed with solder to make them airtight.

People have been trying to preserve food for thousands of years. Some foods, such as fish or beef, can be salted or dried. Large homes used to have ice houses in their grounds where meat and fish could be stored in ice.

▼ Various meats are being preserved in this mid-nineteenth-century cannery.

Typewriter

In the nineteenth century, offices were dominated by clerks. These people sat at high desks and wrote everything out laboriously by hand. Orders, invoices, business letters and reports were all written with pen and ink.

Over the years, many people had tried to invent a machine that would make this work easier and faster, and produce more businesslike results. As early as 1714, a British engineer, Henry Mill, was granted a patent for a writing machine, but no drawings of this have survived.

It was an American who designed the first practical typewriter. In the 1860s, Christopher Latham Sholes and Carlos Glidden were trying to make a machine to number book pages automatically. Suddenly, Glidden turned to Sholes and asked why the machine shouldn't print the words in the book as well. Sholes rose to the challenge and produced a wooden model of a typewriter. It had a keyboard, typebars and an inked ribbon, like millions of machines that came after.

The Remington company, an arms manufacturer, saw the potential of Sholes' design and bought the rights to manufacture it. They began production in 1873, and within three years typewriters were being sold in their thousands. Clerks began to be replaced by secretaries, and business letters changed their appearance for good.

Typewriters vary from one place to another, because of the different scripts and alphabets used around the world. Most typewriters have about fifty keys, but Chinese typewriters have a single key and a number of trays containing, in total, around 3,000 characters.

◀ By 1927, when this advertisement of the Italian Olivetti company was produced, typewriters were common in offices throughout Europe and America.

Sewing machine

In 1830, French tailor Barthélémy Thimonnier was excited. He had designed a machine to help him with his sewing! Before this, Thimonnier and every other tailor sewed everything by hand, with a needle and thread. The new machine, Thimonnier thought, would make him rich. He would be able to turn out clothes much faster and more easily than anyone else.

In 1831, Thimonnier set up a workshop in Paris to make military uniforms. To begin with, everything went well. The sewing machines, made mostly of wood, were rather cumbersome, but they had most of the features of the modern sewing machine. However, other garment-makers got to hear of Thimonnier's success. They feared that the new machines would put them out of a job. They attacked his workshop, and wrecked it. Thimonnier escaped and fled Paris. He carried on improving his sewing machine, taking out further patents. But he never made much money from his invention and was a poor man when he died in 1857.

It was left to American inventors, such as Walter Hunt (see page 50) and Elias Howe, to develop the sewing machine. Both of these inventors made large machines for use in factories. But it was Isaac Merrit Singer of Massachusetts who made the first small sewing machine for home use. Singer's machines caught on quickly, and they were soon seen all over America.

Singer's machine was successful because his company developed ways of making it cheaply. Singer's company was one of the pioneers of mass-production techniques.

◀ Singer hand and electric sewing machines were sold all over the world by the time this advertisement was produced in 1930.

Railways

Hauling coal and iron ore out of mines is hard work. Since at least the sixteenth century, some mines had used horse-drawn carts on primitive wooden rails. In 1804, Cornish engineer Richard Trevithick started to use a steam engine to pull the carts. The heavy engine often broke the rails.

Another engineer, George Stephenson, developed steam railways. He saw the advantage of stronger wrought-iron rails, and used them on his new Stockton and Darlington Railway in northern England. This railway had both steam-drawn and horse-drawn trains.

Stephenson also built the first railway to be worked entirely by steam, the Liverpool and Manchester Railway. This line opened in 1830. It had wrought-iron rails and a new locomotive, called the *Rocket*, specially built by Stephenson's son Robert. This railway was a great success: the age of the train had begun.

▲ The Liverpool and Manchester Railway soon proved popular. During the decades after 1830, many other railway services started up in England.

When it was tried out before the opening of the Liverpool and Manchester Railway, the *Rocket* reached a maximum speed of 29 mph (46.7 kph), which was considered enormously fast at the time.

▼ The *Rocket*, the first successful steam locomotive, was the model for many future railway engines in the first half of the nineteenth century.

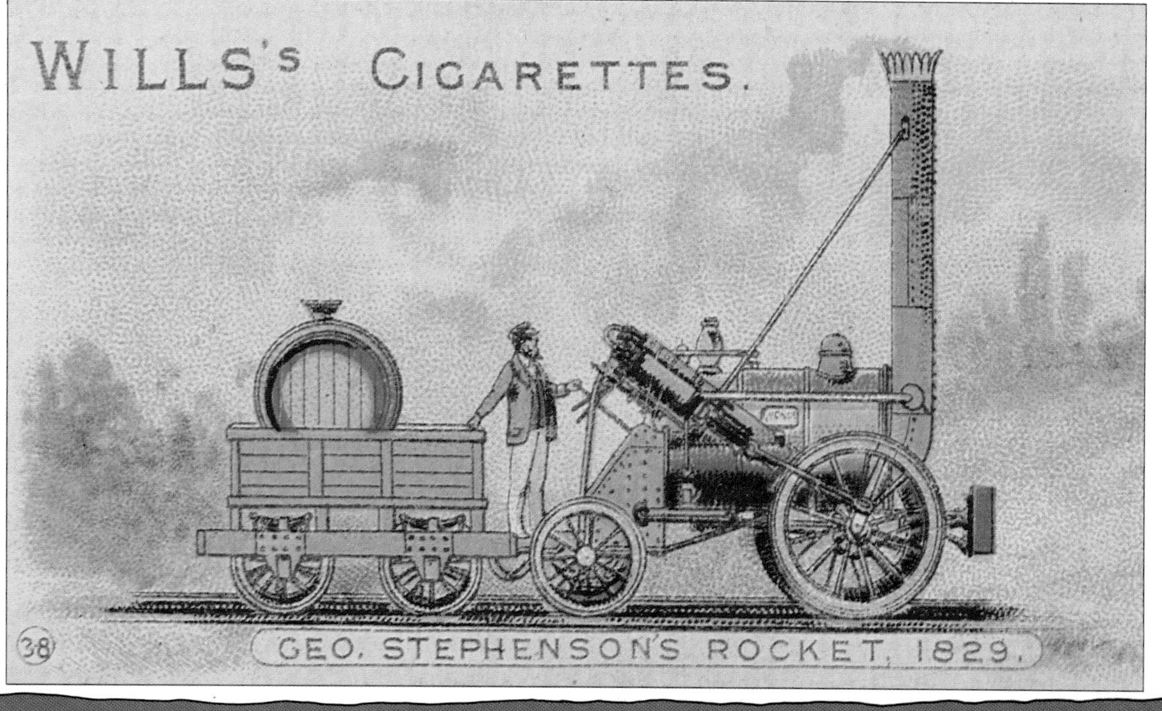

Bicycle

The bicycle seems such a simple invention that we take it for granted. But bicycles have been around for little more than 150 years. In about 1816, a German inventor called Karl Friedrich von Drais produced a machine that was almost a bicycle. It had two wheels and was pushed along by kicking.

In 1839, the true bicycle, powered by pedals, was pioneered by British inventor Kirkpatrick Macmillan. Macmillan's bicycle had a crank that connected the rear wheel with the pedals. French coach-makers Ernest and Pierre Michaux created a similar design in 1861. They also made a machine with pedals attached directly to the front wheel.

None of these bicycles really caught on. The problem was that one push of the pedals turned the wheel only once, so pedalling was hard work. One way of making the machine easier to pedal was to make the front wheel really big. Then, one push of the pedals would send the bicycle much further. This was the idea behind the 'pennyfarthing', or 'ordinary bicycle', produced by English manufacturer James Starley in 1870. It was wobbly, and hard to stop, but it became very popular.

But more successful still was Starley's 'safety bicycle' built in 1885 which was the first bicycle with an efficient chain drive. It could go quickly with little effort, and its smaller wheels were more stable. People have taken to bicycles in their millions ever since.

The idea of the chain drive was illustrated by Leonardo da Vinci (see page 82) in his sketchbooks in the fifteenth century, but was only applied to the bicycle in 1885.

◀ With its high seat and big front wheel, the pennyfarthing was difficult to balance. But people liked it because it was not too hard to pedal.

Underground railways

In the mid-nineteenth century, London was growing faster than any city before. The centre of a huge empire, it almost exploded as thousands of new houses, shops, offices and factories were built for the expanding workforce. These people needed better transport than the narrow streets could offer.

Charles Pearson saw that the answer was to build railways underground. He put his proposal to Parliament in 1843, but the short Metropolitan Railway did not open until 1863. But even over this 4-mile (6.5-km) route, the line was very successful, with 9.5 million passengers using it in the first year. Other cities soon followed London. Budapest's underground opened in 1896, Boston's subway in 1897, the Paris métro in 1900 and New York's subway in 1904.

The first underground lines were made by the 'cut-and-cover' process: digging a deep trench and covering the top. True 'tube' railways, made by boring through the earth using a steel ring pushed by a hydraulic ram, followed in 1890.

▼ By 1915, London's underground was beginning to grow into quite a large network.

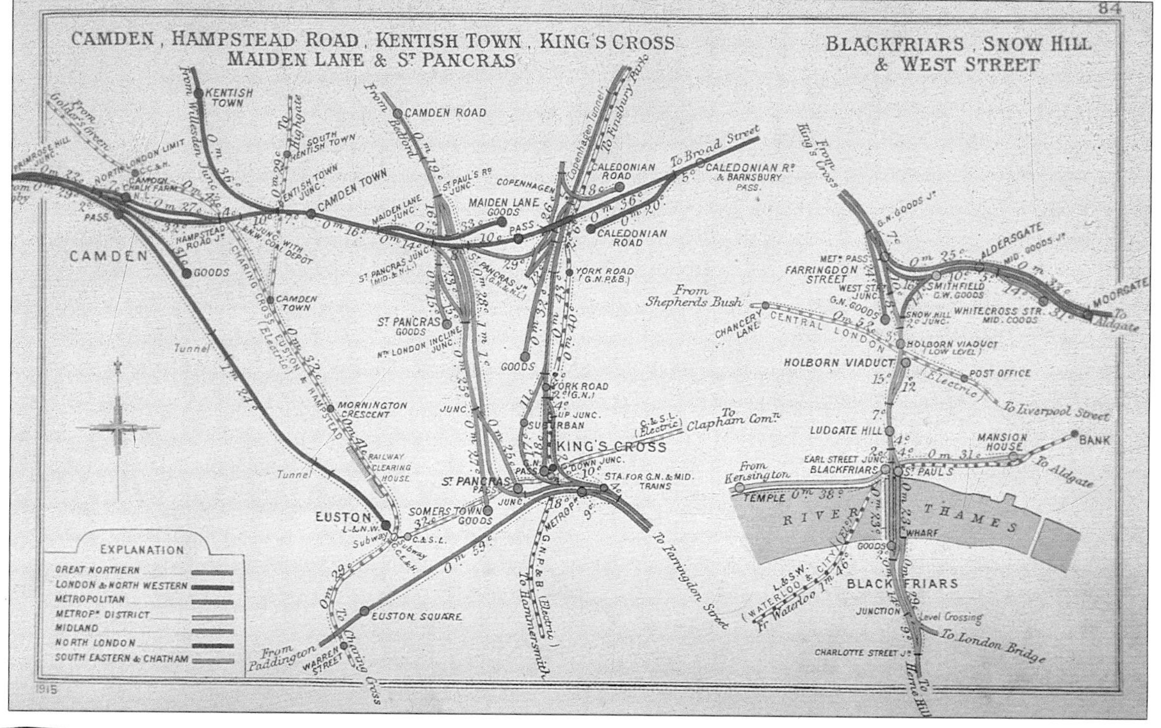

Ship's propeller

What was the best way to drive a steam ship? The first experiments were with paddlesteamers. But some people liked the more efficient screw propeller. Swedish ex-army officer John Ericsson and British engineer Francis Pettit Smith both designed screw-propelled ships in the 1830s. They got their idea from the ancient Greeks, who used the Archimedes' screw (see page 21), a device like a corkscrew in a tube, to raise water.

Pettit Smith's trials were successful, but not in quite the way he intended. He built a ship with a wooden propeller, part of which broke off. To his surprise, the ship went faster with the shortened propeller! So he built another ship, the *Archimedes*, which was launched in 1838. Pettit Smith's work was watched with interest by the engineer Isambard Kingdom Brunel, who was building a huge steamship, the *Great Britain*. Brunel planned to use paddle wheels on the *Great Britain*, but changed to propellers when he saw the *Archimedes*. Once people saw the success of Brunel's large ship, which made its first Atlantic crossing in 1845, propeller-driven vessels became more and more popular.

▲ When the *Great Britain* ran aground in 1846, her huge hull and her screw propeller were clearly visible. In spite of this incident, the ship was very successful, and many other ships soon boasted efficient screw propellers.

In 1845, a paddlesteamer and a propeller-powered ship took part in a tug of war. The ship with the propeller won easily.

◀ Like many vessels of her time, the *Great Britain* had sails as well as steam engines. When there was a favourable wind she could sail quickly, saving her fuel for when it was calm or when the wind was blowing in the wrong direction.

Air-filled tyre

In the ancient world, carts rattled along on wooden wheels. When the cart hit a bump in the road, cargo and passengers could go flying. Later metal wheels were not much better, although things were helped by the suspension systems that were built into vehicles like stagecoaches in the nineteenth century.

Nineteenth-century engineers saw that the answer lay with rubber. They made solid rubber tyres to line the rims of wheels. These provided a cushion against some of the bumps and helped the wheels grip the road.

Two inventors had ideas for inflatable tyres in the nineteenth century. Robert Thompson designed a leather tyre and patented it in 1845. But the successful design was produced by Scotsman John Dunlop in 1887.

Dunlop's son had complained when his tricycle broke as a result of the pounding it got on the cobbled streets. Dunlop came up with a tyre that was inflated with air through a valve. When the tyre was wrapped around the wheel, it looked rather like an Egyptian mummy. To begin with, people laughed at Dunlop's 'mummy tyres'. But they found favour with cyclists – especially racing cyclists, who realized they could go faster with the new tyres fitted.

One invention that made air-filled tyres more practical was the concave, or dished, wheel rim, which helps keep the tyre on the wheel. This innovation was patented by British engineer C. K. Welch in 1890.

▶ Different kinds of air-filled tyres are made for every conceivable type of vehicle. This enormous truck tyre was the world's largest when it was made in 1946. Today, even bigger ones are made.

Safety pin

Before there were zips, buttons or other fastenings, our ancestors fastened their clothes together with large pins. But pins caused problems. Their sharp points were dangerous, and they could easily slip out.

Someone, perhaps on the island of Crete about 4,000 years ago, found a brilliant solution to these problems by making devices that looked like large safety pins to fasten garments. The bronze pins were doubled over, with a catch at one end to secure the point. Later pins also had a spring, so that they held firm.

But by the nineteenth century, people had forgotten about the ancient pin, until Walter Hunt (see also page 44) invented the modern safety pin in 1849. Hunt thought up many inventions, which he usually patented. Since a patent application normally included drawings, Hunt was usually in debt to his artist. He agreed to wipe out the debt by giving the artist the rights to whatever Hunt could make out of a length of old wire. Hunt came up with the safety pin, such a good invention that the artist, a man named Richardson, actually paid Hunt $400 for it. Hunt was pleased, but he had still sold his invention cheaply.

▲ This sixth-century brooch is fastened by the pin that passes across the middle – just like a modern safety pin.

Many ancient peoples, from the Greeks and Romans to the Celts of ancient Britain, used the ancient form of the safety pin. The pins were often highly decorated, so that they were more like brooches than pins.

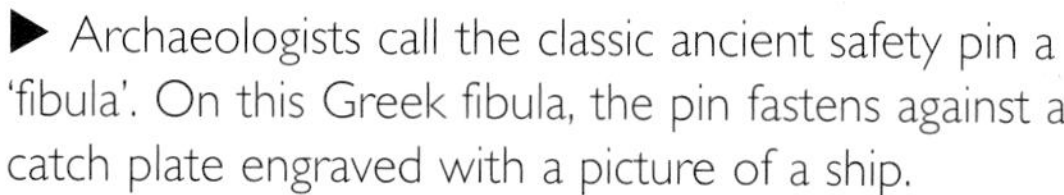

▶ Archaeologists call the classic ancient safety pin a 'fibula'. On this Greek fibula, the pin fastens against a catch plate engraved with a picture of a ship.

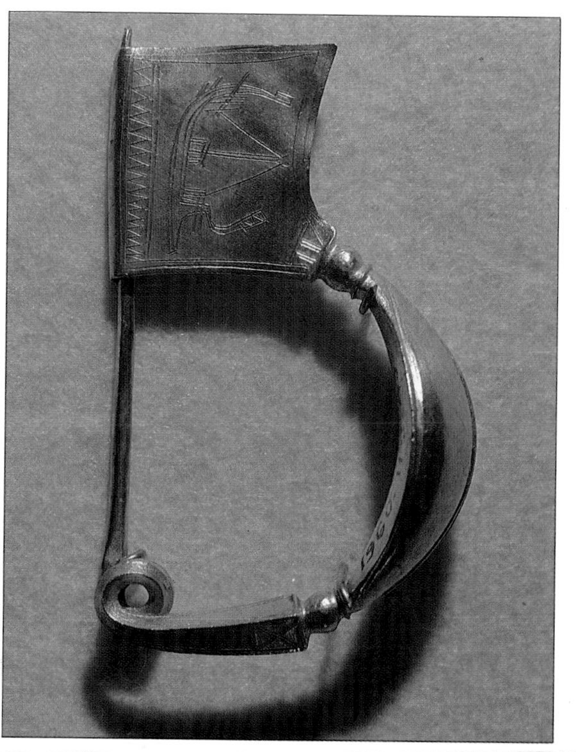

▼ In the early twentieth century, safety pins were sold as cheap, useful items. Small ones only cost 2 cents for a dozen – a far cry from ancient bronze fibulae!

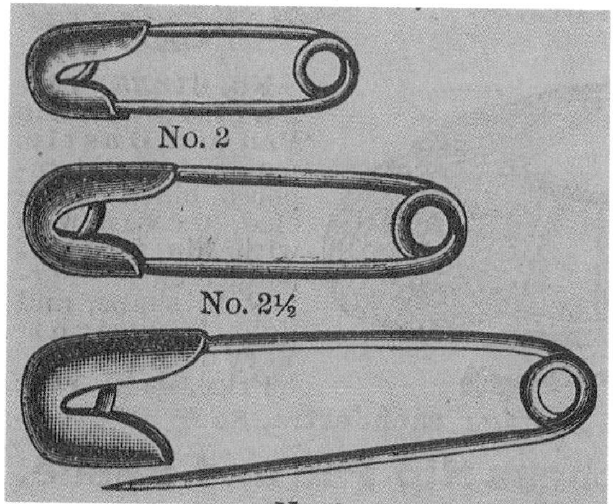

Elevator

Builders have been able to make tall structures for hundreds of years, as the church spires of the the Middle Ages show. But one thing stopped them building tall structures for people to live and work in: the stairs. There was no point living sixty floors up, if you had to climb all the way up to your apartment. Of course, there were simple lifts or hoists with a platform pulled up by a rope running over a pulley. But if the rope broke, the passengers would fall, so hoists like this were used only for goods.

The man who changed all this was an American mechanic called Elisha Graves Otis. His invention was simple: a ratchet mechanism that 'caught' the elevator cage if the rope snapped, so that it would fall at most a few feet. Otis set up his stand at a New York trade exhibition in 1854. When he had a large enough audience, he stepped into his elevator and asked someone to cut the cable. The elevator only dropped a couple of inches. Safe elevators had come to stay.

Modern elevators need to be fast as well as reliable. Those in New York's Empire State Building, for example, travel at up to 1,200 ft (366 m) per minute. Elevators in newer skyscrapers move even faster.

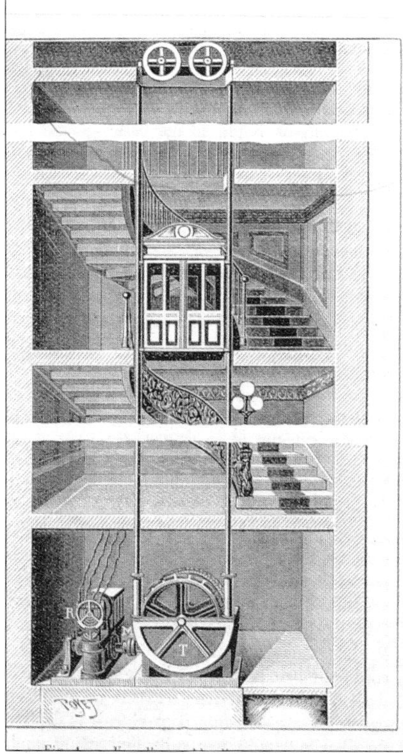

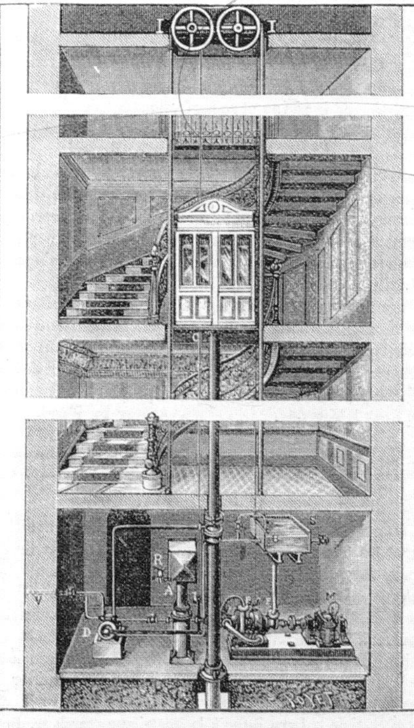

◀ By the end of the nineteenth century, elevators were common in office and apartment blocks. Both electric (far left) and hydraulic (left) mechanisms were being used to power the elevator cages.

Refrigerator

Today, every home has a refrigerator to keep food fresh. People have long known that a cool environment is best for preserving food. But until the end of the nineteenth century only the rich, with purpose-built ice houses, could take advantage of this. A cool larder was the best most people could hope for.

Jacob Perkins, an American working in England, made the discovery that led to refrigeration. In 1834, he found that there is a cooling effect when certain liquids are evaporated. Perkins asked a group of mechanics to make a working model to demonstrate the idea. Sure enough, one evening the device actually produced some ice. The mechanics were so excited that they took the ice, jumped in a cab and raced to Perkins' house to show him the successful result.

Perkins, by now an elderly man, did not market his invention. The man who did was John Harrison, a Scottish printer who lived in Australia. Harrison probably discovered the cooling effect without knowing of Perkins' work. He used ether to clean his metal printing type, and one day noticed the cooling effect of the substance. By 1862, his first refrigerators were on sale and Harrison had installed the first refrigeration plant in a brewery in Bendigo, Victoria.

▲ Harrison's work paved the way for early home refrigerators like these. Soon the units would be smaller and would fit more easily into the kitchen.

German engineer Carl von Linde produced the first domestic refrigerator in 1879. But refrigeration did not come into the home on a large scale until the invention of electric refrigerators in the 1920s.

▶ One of the most important uses for refrigerators was on board ships. Large cold stores meant that ships could carry meat over long distances – allowing lamb to be exported from New Zealand to Europe, for example.

Barbed wire

In the mid-nineteenth century, people were beginning to settle on the Great Plains of the USA. It was a chance for small farmers to start up on their own. But they were hampered by large-scale cattle ranchers, who would drive their herds over the settlers' fields. Ordinary fences were not strong enough to keep them out. The solution was for the settlers to fence off their land with barbed wire. This was first patented by American inventor Lucien B. Smith in 1867. But as yet no one had invented a machine that could produce the wire quickly and cheaply.

In 1873, two friends, Joseph F. Glidden and Jacob Haish, decided to devise a machine to make the wire without telling the other. Glidden finished his machine first and patented it before the end of the year. He made a great deal of money from his invention, but fell out with Haish, who felt that he had been cheated by Glidden when he got to the patent office first.

▲ This farmer is using a metal bar to pull a length of barbed wire taut before fixing it to a fence post. By doing this, he is ensuring that his fence will not sag.

Barbed wire was also used in war. British Field Marshal Kitchener used it during the Boer War to restrict his Boer guerrilla enemies. Miles of it were used in Europe, in and around the trenches, during World War I.

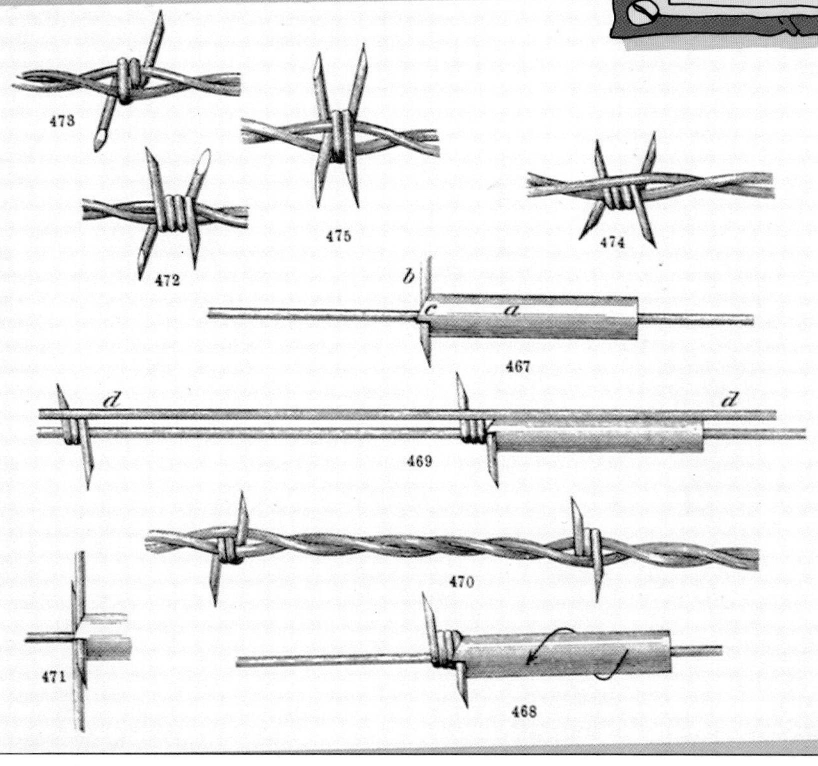

◀ Many different types of barbed wire were made with barbs in various shapes to repel the cattle. But the person who made most money from barbed wire was Glidden, the man who perfected a machine to produce the wire cheaply.

Margarine

In 1869, the French emperor Napoleon III announced a competition for a replacement for butter, because shortages of animal fat had pushed up the price of butter. The Emperor was also thinking of feeding his troops, and butter, which could easily melt or turn rancid, was not ideal for taking on military campaign.

French chemist Hippolyte Mège-Mouriès took up the challenge. He processed beef tallow to create a fat he called 'oleo'. This he liquefied and mixed with milk and water. Finally, he added pieces of finely chopped cow's udder. The pearl-like colour of the resulting mix suggested to Mège-Mouriès the name margarine, from the Greek 'margaron', meaning pearl. Margarine was not sold widely to begin with. But in the twentieth century, as butter got more costly, margarine became more successful.

▲ Early margarine was hard and difficult to spread. An important breakthrough was easy-to-spread, soft margarine, which appeared in the early 1970s.

Mège-Mouriès did not profit greatly from his invention. He was taken prisoner in the Franco-Prussian War in 1870, retired to England, and died there in poverty in 1883. Soon after this, margarine became more popular.

Plastics

It was a photographer's experiments in the darkroom that led to the first plastic. Photography was one of Alexander Parkes' many interests. In the nineteenth century, you could not just buy photographic films and chemicals off the shelf as you can today. You had to make what was needed yourself. So every photographer had to be a chemist too. One of the substances used in photography was 'collodion', a solution of 'guncotton', or cellulose nitrate, in alcohol and ether, which was used to stick light-sensitive chemicals to a glass plate to make the nineteenth-century equivalent of a photographic film.

In the 1850s, Parkes looked at different ways of treating the collodion. One day, he tried mixing it with camphor. To his surprise, it produced a hard, flexible material. Parkes called his substance 'Parkesine', and it was the first plastic. Parkes made all sorts of objects out of Parkesine: combs, pens, buttons, and jewellery. However, Parkes had little business sense, and lost money on his new venture.

It was left to other inventors to build on Parkes' work and make money out of it. John Wesley Hyatt, a printer from New York, saw the chance in 1868, when a company making billiard balls complained that there was a shortage of ivory. Hyatt improved the manufacturing process and gave Parkesine a new name: 'celluloid'. He had a ready market from the billiard ball manufacturers, and soon a huge variety of items was being made out of plastic.

Early plastics caught fire easily, which limited the range of items that could be made with them. The first successful plastic that would withstand high temperatures was 'Bakelite', patented by Leo Baekeland in 1909.

◀ During the twentieth century, people began to discover new uses for plastics. Almost any item in the home could be made of some sort of plastic.

Stapler

Every office has at least one stapler. It provides the ideal way of joining a number of papers together and keeping them together. But the first stapler was not an office product at all. It was developed for the printing industry.

The traditional way to bind a book involves sewing the pages together in groups called 'signatures'. This is quite a complex process, straightforward for a trained bookbinder, but difficult for a machine. So binders who wanted to speed up the process, especially to produce booklets and magazines, which are usually wanted quickly, tried to find a way of binding using short pieces of bent wire.

In 1869, Thomas Briggs of Boston, Massachusetts, invented a machine that would do this. He started a company, the Boston Wire Stitcher Company, to make and market the machines. His machine cut the wire and bent it into a U-shape, drove it through the paper, and bent it again to fix the papers in place.

Briggs' first machine was rather complicated, because it carried out so many operations. So in 1894, he came up with a process in which the wire was cut and bent first to produce a series of staples. These could be loaded into a much simpler machine, which could insert them into the paper. This machine is the ancestor of the staplers used in offices and homes today.

Early staples were wrapped in paper or loaded individually into the stapler. Staplers became much easier to use in the 1920s, when staples glued together in a strip were put on the market.

▼ The present-day stapler combines a container for the staples and the stapling mechanism itself in one neat design.

Traffic signals

Since the early days of the railways, there had been signals to show whether it was safe for a train to travel along a length of track. In 1868, inventor J. P. Knight had the idea of adapting these signals for use on the roads. He set up the first traffic signals outside the Houses of Parliament in London. They were like railway signals, with a tilting arm, and incorporated red and green gas lights for use at night. But when one of the signals blew up and killed a policeman, the idea was abandoned.

With the invention of the motor car and the increase in traffic, there became a need for traffic signals, especially in America. Alfred Benesch developed a system of red and green lights in the early twentieth century, and the first lights were installed in Cleveland, Ohio. Four years later, a third colour, amber, was added to traffic lights that were set up in New York. Traffic signals re-appeared in England in 1925.

Automatic signals were soon developed. Lights controlled by a timer appeared in 1926. Six years later, signals operated by the traffic itself, via pressure pads in the road, were introduced.

Modern traffic signals are often controlled by computers. Linked to traffic detectors beneath the road, the computer monitors the flow of traffic and works out the best times for the lights to change over.

▼ By 1903, when this photograph was taken, traffic in London was already a problem. The mixture of horses, motor vehicles and bicycles was perhaps just as dangerous as today's fast-moving cars.

Carpet sweeper

A man's migraine headaches led to the invention of the carpet sweeper. In the 1870s, Melville Bissell worked in a porcelain factory in Grand Rapids, Michigan. The china was packed in straw that produced clouds of dust. The dust was even worse when the workers set to and swept the packing room with ordinary brooms. And it was at these times that Bissell's headaches got worse. He began to realize that his illness was probably due to an allergic reaction to dust. A device that kept both brush and dust inside a box was the obvious answer to Bissell's problems, so he set to work to design it.

After experimenting with a number of designs, he decided on a series of brushes attached to a cylinder. The cylinder was connected to the sweeper's wheels, so would turn when the sweeper was pushed along. There was a knob that could adjust the height of the brushes to cope with different types of floor surface. And, most importantly of all, the whole mechanism was housed in a box that also collected the dust. In 1876, Bissell put his 'Grand Rapids' carpet sweeper on the market.

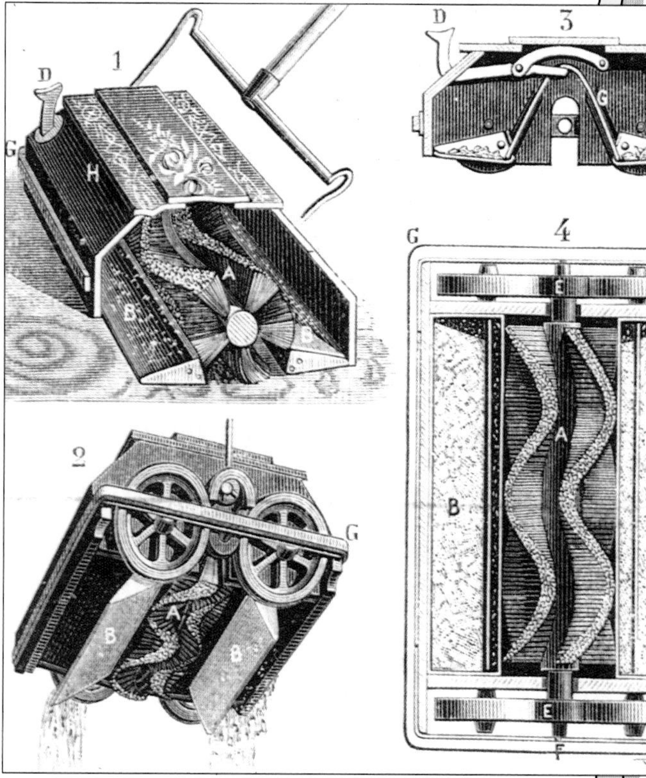

▲ Spiral rotating brushes swept the dust up into Bissell's sweeper. Two folding lids could be pulled down to empty the sweeper when it was full.

Before the invention of the carpet sweeper, people used to clean carpets by sprinkling tea leaves on the floor and sweeping up the mess with a broom. Some of the dust landed in the dust-pan, but much of it fell back on to the carpet.

Bissell's sweeper was an immediate success. It was quicker, easier and cleaner to use than a broom. It was also a simple, fairly cheap design that many people could afford. Even after the arrival of the vacuum cleaner in the 1900s, many people still swept their carpets with the machine that cured Bissell of his headaches.

◀ This much-used Grand Rapids sweeper was one of the first that Bissell produced.

Telephone

People have always wanted to communicate with others who are out of earshot. The ancient Romans flashed mirrors from hilltop to hilltop, and many other peoples have used bonfires and smoke signals. But the man who invented the telephone was not at first interested in this problem at all.

Alexander Graham Bell (see also pages 77 and 84) was a Scottish doctor who worked with the deaf in North America. His work naturally led him to the study of sound, and to an interest in how sound could be transmitted electrically.

Bell used a 'diaphragm', or membrane, that would vibrate in response to the human voice. This was arranged next to an electromagnet, so that the vibrations of the diaphragm would lead to changes in the magnetic field and, in turn, to variations in the electric current in a wire. At the receiving end, the current could be turned back into vibrations and sound waves by a similar device. In 1876, Bell sent the first telephone message to his assistant in the same building: 'Mr Watson, come here. I want you.' The following years saw telephone cables stretching across North America.

▲ Alexander Graham Bell demonstrates his telephone. As he speaks into the unit, the onlookers wait to hear the reply.

The earliest telephones did not have dials. All calls had to be made through the operator, who connected the caller with the correct line. Dials appeared in the early twentieth century, allowing some numbers to be contacted automatically.

▼ As the telephone network grew, exchanges like this became common. By pushing pegs into the boards, different telephones were linked together.

Electric light bulb

Every day, we switch on lights without thinking about it. Yet the electric light bulb, which was to change the face of cities and bring safe light into every home, was invented less than 120 years ago.

Many scientists worked on ideas for electric lighting, but the invention of the light bulb turned out to be a race between two men. Englishman Joseph Swan (see also page 62) was working on the idea from about 1860. American Thomas Alva Edison began to investigate electric lighting in the 1870s. They both had the same idea of passing a current through a 'filament' or thread of cotton which had been scorched to form carbon. The filament glowed when the current was switched on. Sometimes the carbon burned through too quickly, and sometimes the glass bulb containing the filament broke. But by 1880, both men had developed efficient, lasting bulbs. Edison, with a natural flair for publicity, had street lights installed in his home town of Menlo Park, New Jersey. By 1882, his bulbs were lighting an area of New York City.

To begin with, Swan and Edison worked in competition. But by 1883 they had joined forces, forming the Edison and Swan United Electric Light Company. Their work led to the 'all-electric' homes of today.

▲ A poster advertising light bulbs shows the City of London illuminated at night.

Before the invention of the electric light bulb, there was no industry generating electricity for use in the home. Only when cheap electric lighting became available did companies think it was worthwhile generating electricity and building power supply lines.

◀ An early window display in a New York City shop shows the figure of Thomas Edison together with many examples of his invention. In the USA, no one had heard of Swan, so the picture of the famous American inventor was used to help sell the bulbs.

Electric iron

The electric iron is a good example of an invention arriving before its time. Europeans have ironed their clothes since the seventeenth century. They did this with a heavy 'flat iron', which had to be heated up in a fire or on a hot-plate. This caused all sorts of problems. It was easy to get the iron too hot, and scorch the clothes. Anxiety about doing this meant that it was equally easy to try to begin when the iron had not warmed up properly. The handle of the iron also got very hot, meaning that people often burned themselves while ironing.

Hollow irons, filled with hot water or hot embers, introduced in the nineteenth century, were only a little better.

New York inventor Henry W. Seeley was the man who changed all this. He invented the first practical electric iron in 1882. It contained a wire element that heated up when an electric current passed through it, the same principle as the traditional electric cooker hotplate.

The problem with Seeley's iron was that when it appeared, very few homes had electricity, so many people continued using flat irons well into the twentieth century.

▲ This French electric iron was made in around 1906. It was a very simple device, with none of the different heat settings that are available on a modern iron. This meant that is was hardly any easier to use than the old-fashioned flat iron – except that you did not have to heat it up in the fire first.

The first steam iron, in which a jet of steam is produced to moisten the material that is being ironed, appeared in 1926 in New York. It was manufactured by a company called Eldec.

▶ Today, most people use a steam iron. This delivers a jet of steam through the plate on the base of the iron and makes ironing easier and quicker.

Artificial fibres

▲ The cellulose nitrate was washed then dissolved in alcohol and ether to form a substance called collodion, which could be extruded into the artificial fibre rayon.

In 1644, British scientist Robert Hooke wrote that it ought to be possible for humans to imitate the process that the silk moth uses to produce silk. But Hooke never followed up his idea.

One inventor who came close was British scientist Joseph Swan (see page 60). In 1883, he was working on the invention for which he is remembered: the electric light bulb. He was trying out materials for the filament, the thread that glows in the bulb. He worked out that if he mixed cellulose nitrate and acetic acid, and 'extruded', or forced, the mixture through a series of tiny holes, he would make a fibre.

Swan did not realize the importance of his new fibre, and went on with his work on the light bulb. But at the same time, French Count Hilaire de Chardonnet was also extruding cellulose nitrate through holes to create a continuous filament. Chardonnet called his fibre 'artificial silk'. It was later known as 'rayon'. From the 1940s, rayon was gradually replaced by the versatile artificial fibre nylon. This was invented by a team from the Du Pont company led by Wallace H. Carothers. Nylon is used for everything: from ropes to boat sails, stockings to fishing nets.

Nylon is now also made in a solid form, to form sheet materials and mouldings. In this form, nylon is used to make many different items, such as gearwheels and wire insulation.

Fountain pen

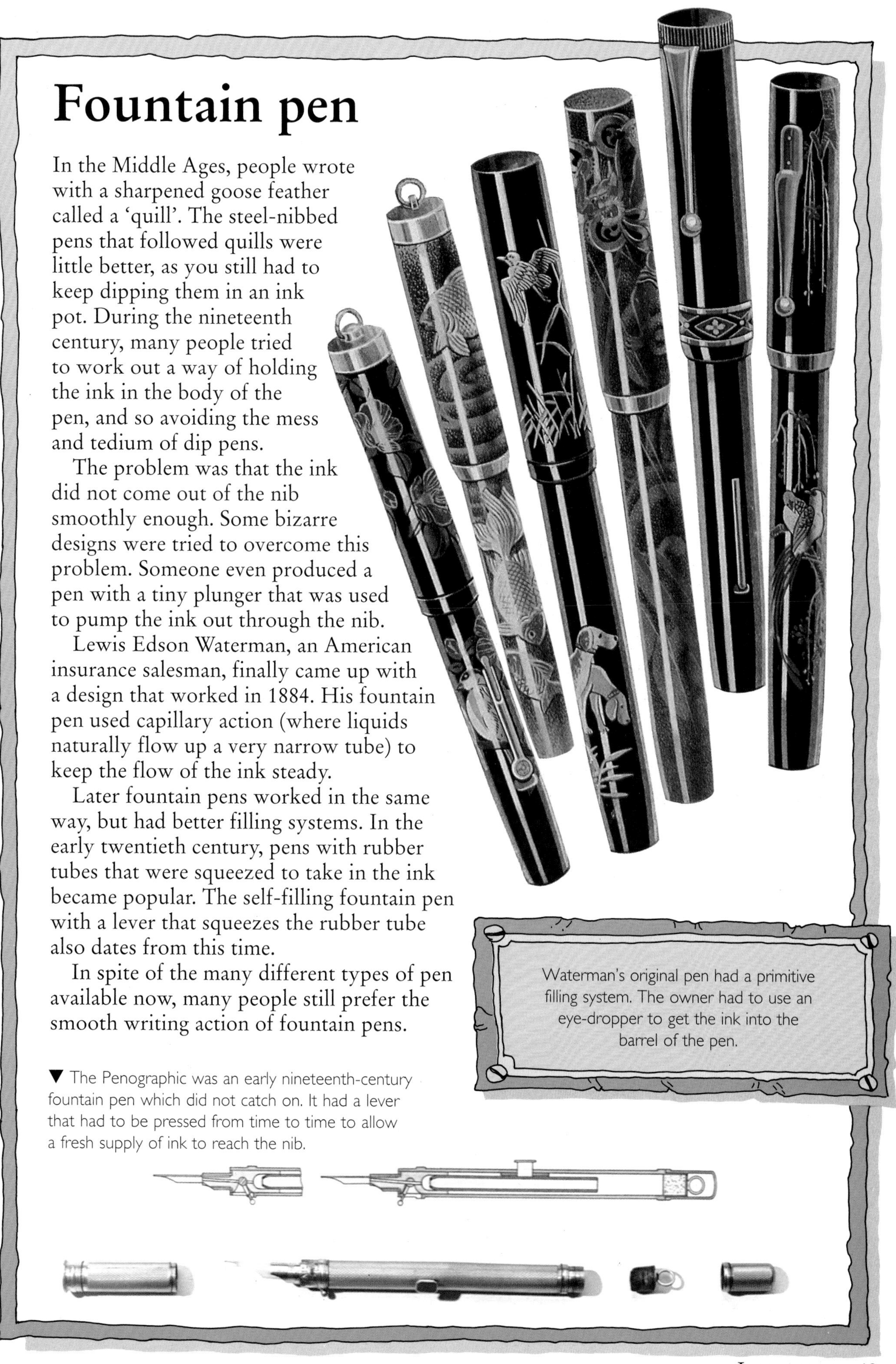

In the Middle Ages, people wrote with a sharpened goose feather called a 'quill'. The steel-nibbed pens that followed quills were little better, as you still had to keep dipping them in an ink pot. During the nineteenth century, many people tried to work out a way of holding the ink in the body of the pen, and so avoiding the mess and tedium of dip pens.

The problem was that the ink did not come out of the nib smoothly enough. Some bizarre designs were tried to overcome this problem. Someone even produced a pen with a tiny plunger that was used to pump the ink out through the nib.

Lewis Edson Waterman, an American insurance salesman, finally came up with a design that worked in 1884. His fountain pen used capillary action (where liquids naturally flow up a very narrow tube) to keep the flow of the ink steady.

Later fountain pens worked in the same way, but had better filling systems. In the early twentieth century, pens with rubber tubes that were squeezed to take in the ink became popular. The self-filling fountain pen with a lever that squeezes the rubber tube also dates from this time.

In spite of the many different types of pen available now, many people still prefer the smooth writing action of fountain pens.

Waterman's original pen had a primitive filling system. The owner had to use an eye-dropper to get the ink into the barrel of the pen.

▼ The Penographic was an early nineteenth-century fountain pen which did not catch on. It had a lever that had to be pressed from time to time to allow a fresh supply of ink to reach the nib.

Motor car and motorcycle

Gottlieb Daimler of Württemberg, Germany, worked in a factory making early internal combustion engines. In the 1880s, he experimented with engines of his own. But unlike the heavy engines in the factory, which were fuelled with town gas and drove stationary machines, Daimler's engine was a lightweight design, fuelled with petrol. In 1885, he connected one of his petrol engines to a bicycle. The following year he was a terrifying sight riding about the streets.

Carl Benz of Mannheim was another man who wanted to use petrol engines in transport. While Daimler was roaring around on his motorcycle, Benz fitted a petrol engine to a three-wheeled vehicle in 1886. It was the first motor car.

That first 1886 Benz car had bicycle wheels, was steered with a tiller like a boat, and had a high stagecoach-style seat. By 1893, Benz had produced a more familiar-looking four-wheeled car.

All of these early vehicles were hand-made, very expensive, travelled very slowly and often broke down. But they were the beginning of a revolution that brought motor transport to all.

Early Benz cars travelled at around 8 mph (13 kph). In spite of the slow speed of early cars, people were terrified of them. In England, a man with a red flag had to walk in front, warning people of the car's arrival!

▼ A motor car of 1903 roars through an English village. The driver and passengers had to wear warm clothes in the drafty, open vehicle.

Vacuum flask

The idea behind the vacuum flask is simple. The flask has an inner and an outer wall. Between these two walls is a vacuum, which is a space that is completely empty (even without air inside). Heat cannot be transferred across a vacuum, so any liquid poured into the flask stays at its original temperature for a long time. This is why a vacuum flask can keep hot drinks warm in winter or cold liquids cool in summer. Many people who do a lot of travelling find it difficult to imagine life without a flask.

But the vacuum flask was only invented in 1892, and even then its inventor did not realize how useful it could be. The inventor was Scottish scientist Sir James Dewar. However, it was German glass-worker Reinhold Burger who realized that the vacuum flask would be useful in all kinds of situations. He patented the vacuum flask in 1903, and made plans to put it on the market. Burger even held a competition to find a good name for the flask. The winner he chose was 'Thermos', which is the Greek word for hot. Burger's product was very successful, and he was soon exporting his vacuum flasks all over the world.

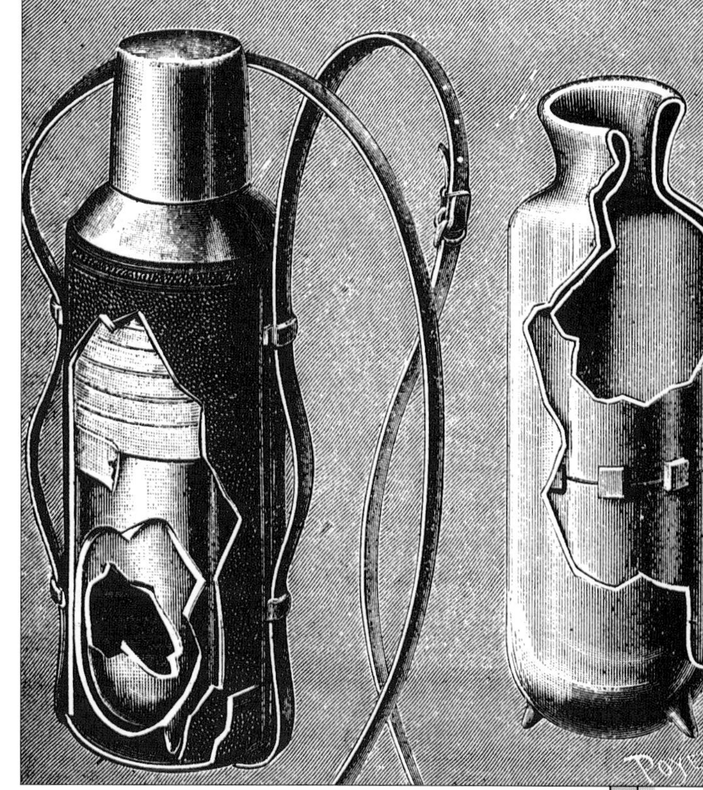

Vacuum flasks are often used for scientific purposes, for example, when liquids need to be kept at a constant temperature. Vaccines, serums and other liquids are often carried in vacuum flasks.

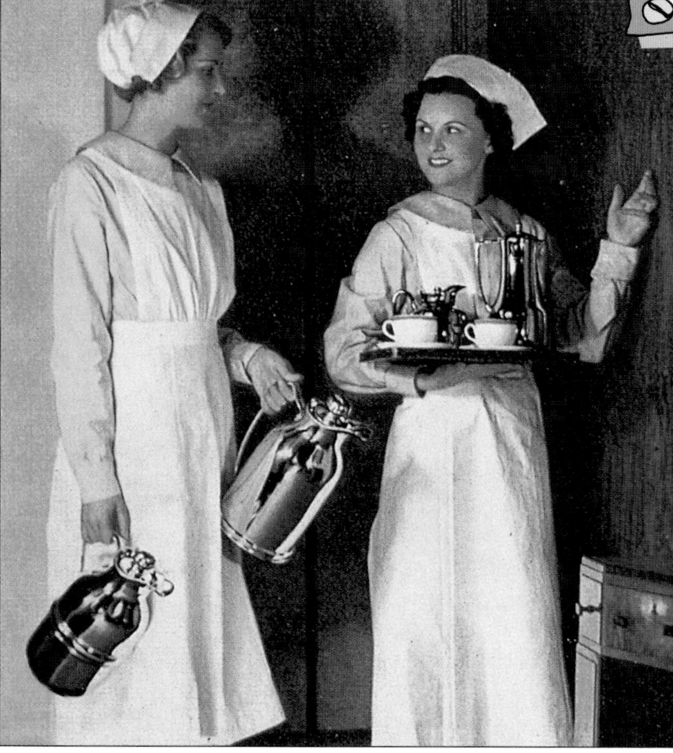

◀ These hotel maids of the 1920s are serving guests their morning coffee in Thermos flasks. If the guests fall asleep again, the coffee will still be piping hot.

Photography

The first surviving photograph was taken by the Frenchman Joseph Nicéphore Niepce in 1827. But it was many years before photography became the simple and straightforward process it is today. To make his photograph, Niepce coated a plate made of pewter with bitumen. The plate was exposed in a camera for several minutes before being treated with chemicals to make the picture emerge slowly on its surface.

During the nineteenth century, inventors tried to improve and simplify photography. They made exposure times much shorter, and found chemicals that produced clearer, sharper images. But photographs were still taken on heavy plates made of metal or glass. The breakthrough came with the work of American George Eastman.

Eastman wanted to create a small camera that was simple to use. In 1884, he developed 'roll-film', a continuous strip of celluloid film, coated with light-sensitive chemicals. Then in 1888 he brought out a new type of camera, which he named the 'Kodak', a name that he hoped would be instantly recognizable in any language. It was the first camera that was truly easy to use. You just pointed the camera, clicked the shutter and wound on. As Eastman said, 'You press the button, we do the rest.'

▲ The first camera made by Niepce was a light-tight wooden box with an opening mechanism on the front called an iris. The plate was inserted in the back of the box and the iris opened to take the picture. Although it is a far cry from today's cameras, a camera is still basically a light-tight box.

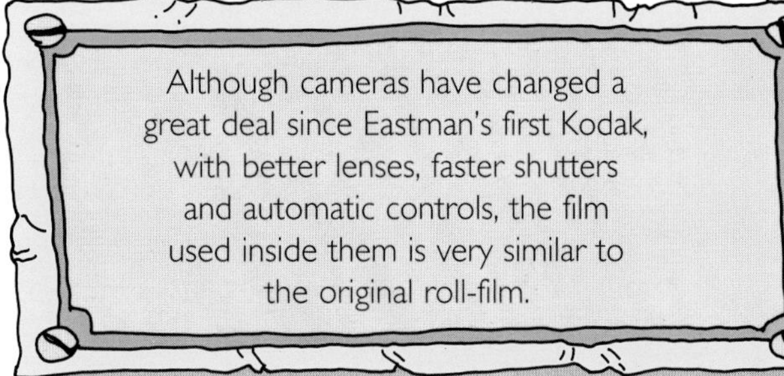

Although cameras have changed a great deal since Eastman's first Kodak, with better lenses, faster shutters and automatic controls, the film used inside them is very similar to the original roll-film.

◀ As Eastman hoped, the name Kodak was soon widely recognized, and Kodak films and cameras were available all over the world.

Escalator

The USA, home of the skyscraper and the safety elevator (see page 51), was also the birthplace of the escalator. Two men created the escalator, Jesse W. Reno and George H. Wheeler. Their first idea was to design a moving slope. This was fairly straightforward to make, but promised to be rather unsettling and even dangerous for the people who rode on it.

So Reno and Wheeler changed their design, replacing the slope with moving steps. The moving stairway was patented in 1892, but was not given the name 'escalator' until 1899. Each step was carried on four wheels which ran on a hidden track beneath. The track levelled out at the top and bottom of the escalator, to enable people to walk on and off the steps. The steps made up a continuous turning loop, just as they do on escalators today.

▲ The first escalator was installed in a hall at the 1900 Universal Exhibition in Paris. Department stores and other businesses were soon ordering escalators for their own buildings.

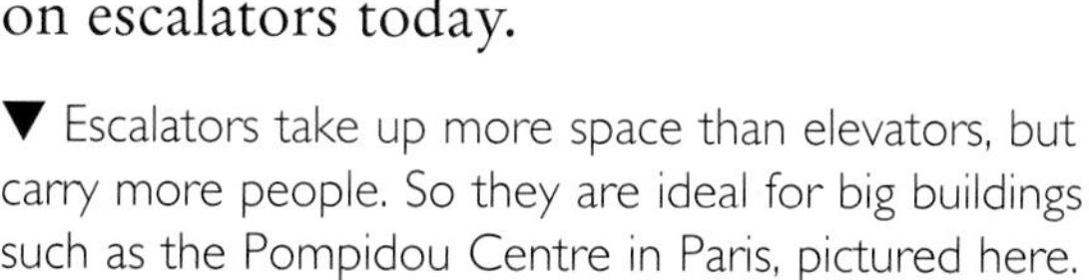

▼ Escalators take up more space than elevators, but carry more people. So they are ideal for big buildings such as the Pompidou Centre in Paris, pictured here.

The 'travelator' is a variation on the escalator. It consists of a moving flat walkway. It is used mainly in airports, where people have to walk long distances on foot often carrying heavy baggage.

Cash register

The cash register provides a way of displaying and recording sales in a shop, particularly the amounts of money that change hands. This invention transformed the way shops were run. It made calculations easy, and showed the customer the exact total to pay. Modern cash registers also print out details of the goods that have been sold on a receipt for the customer, as well as keeping a record of the transaction.

The first cash register was a mechanical device operated by metal keys and containing a mechanism of cogs and levers. It was invented by the American W. S. Burroughs in 1892. Burroughs based his idea on mechanical adding machines that had been developed in 1880 by another American, Hermann Hollerith.

Burroughs died in 1898, before his invention caught on. His company did not make much money from it. But the invention was soon taken up by companies such as the NCR (National Cash Register) Corporation. More than four million machines had been sold by 1950.

Modern cash registers are often connected to a central computer. The cash register can send the computer information about the amount of money taken in the shop and the stock levels of particular items.

Diesel engine

Steam engines, the great power plants of the nineteenth century, were not very efficient. There would be a great prize for the person who came up with a more efficient engine.

German engineer Rudolf Diesel realized that one way to achieve extra efficiency would be to burn the fuel inside the cylinder. This is the idea behind the internal combustion engine. Many such engines had been built during the nineteenth century, but Diesel's design was different.

Diesel kept the heat and pressure as constant as possible inside the cylinder, so more of the heat would be turned into power. This high pressure led to another key feature of his engine. The fuel inside the cylinder of an internal combustion engine has to be ignited, to cause the explosion that makes the piston move. In a petrol engine, this is done with a spark from a spark plug.

▲ Rudolf Diesel relaxes with some of his fellow-engineers at an exhibition of machines at Munich in 1898. This was the exhibition that publicized the German inventor's new form of internal combustion engine for the first time.

In Diesel's engine, the pressure in the cylinder makes the fuel ignite.

In 1892 Diesel patented what he called the 'rational heat engine', what we know as the diesel engine. He demonstrated the engine in 1898 in Munich. It was more efficient than other engines, and was soon being built in large numbers. Today, diesel engines still power lorries, buses, trains, and many cars.

> The efficiency of an engine can be shown by the amount of latent energy that it converts into power. Diesel engines convert at least 35 per cent of the latent fuel energy into power, compared with 28 per cent in a petrol engine and 10 per cent in a steam engine.

◀ Nowadays, diesel engines power heavy vehicles like these buses. In fact, diesel engines are ideal wherever heavy loads need to be hauled and fast acceleration is not required. Taxis also often have diesel engines.

The zip

In the nineteenth century, clothes and many boots and shoes were fastened with buttons. People sometimes had to do up dozens of buttons on the back of a dress or along the side of a boot before they were dressed.

An American engineer called Whitcomb Judson thought he could make matters easier. He invented a new type of fastener. It consisted of a series of clasps that could be opened or closed with a sliding metal guide. He called it his 'clasp locker or unlocker for shoes' and patented it in 1893.

It was a brilliant idea but it did not quite work. Judson's early fastener often stuck, and equally often popped open. Judson worked away at the idea, improving it and inventing machines to manufacture it. But it was not reliable enough and people did not buy it in large numbers.

▲ In the 1980s, the zip became a fashion accessory. Punks wore clothes with zips attached everywhere.

◀ Quick and convenient to use, the zip is now found on virtually every type of garment, wherever hooks and buttons were used in earlier times.

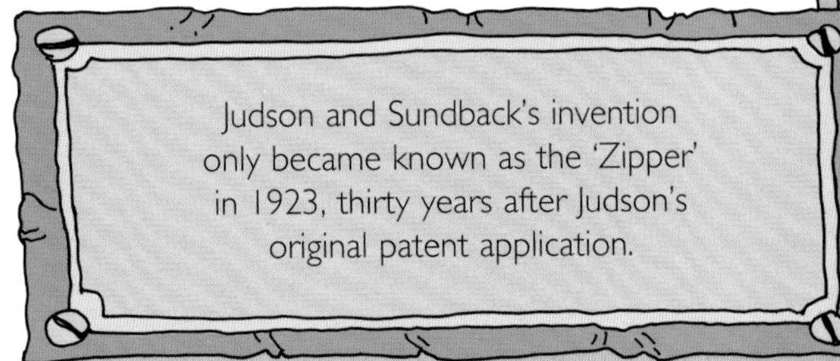

Judson and Sundback's invention only became known as the 'Zipper' in 1923, thirty years after Judson's original patent application.

It took another engineer, Gideon Sundback, to make the final improvements that would make the idea work. Sundback started to work for Judson's company in 1908. He redesigned the links in the fastener several times before coming up with the winning formula in 1913: a cup-shaped link that would be easy to make and fastened easily and reliably. The invention was soon selling in thousands.

Safety razor

King Camp Gillette was a salesman in Wisconsin when his boss threw him a challenge: 'Invent something that will be used once and then thrown away.' They both wanted the customer to come back for more. In 1895, Gillette came up with an idea.

For centuries, men had shaved with large, unwieldy 'cut-throat' razors. These had to be regularly sharpened, and they were dangerous. Gillette's idea was to make a small piece of steel blade that could be fitted in a clamp attached to a handle. When it was blunt, you threw it away and put in another. In other words, the blade would be 'disposable', an unfamiliar word in 1895.

To begin with, there were problems. Steel experts did not think they would be able to produce sharp blades that were thin enough. They also thought that if they could make the blades, they would be so expensive that people would not be able to afford to throw them away! But Gillette stuck to his guns. In 1901, he formed a company to make the new razors. By the following year, they had sorted out most of the manufacturing problems. And by 1904, the blades were selling in their millions.

In 1903, Gillette sold fifty-one razors and 168 blades. By 1904, the figures had risen to 90,000 razors and 12,400,000 blades.

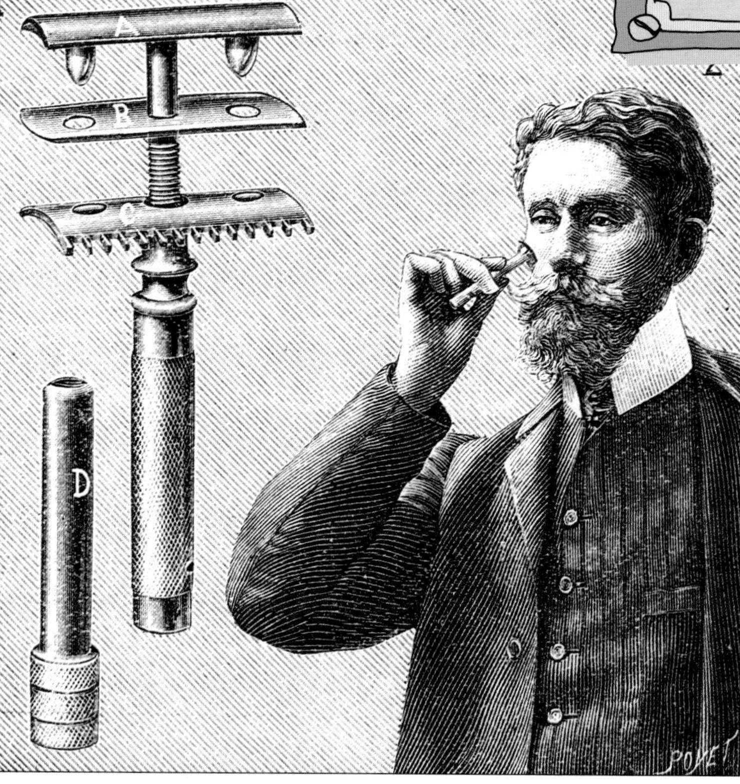

◀ Gillette's safety razor was made with two separate metal plates, between which the thin steel blade was clamped. Screwing the handle together pulled the plates together over the blade, leaving just the sharp edge exposed. It was easy to unscrew the handle and put in a blade when you needed a new one.

Moving pictures

The fascination with moving images goes back thousands of years, and the earliest moving images were probably shadow puppets, moved behind a screen with light shining behind them. In the nineteenth century, people began to take the idea further, and to dream of images that would move without a human operator pulling strings or moving rods.

In 1824, English doctor Peter Mark Roget first noticed an interesting phenomenon that was to make moving images a possibility. This phenomenon, known as 'persistence of vision', means that if you see images of an object in very similar positions in rapid succession, the object seems to move.

Roget's discovery led to many devices that were designed to flash images past the viewer's eyes, giving the illusion of movement. But it was not until the 1880s, that two French brothers, Louis and Auguste Lumière, started work on the first cinema system.

The Lumières developed a machine that took a sequence of pictures on a continuous strip of film. The same device also projected the pictures on to a screen. On 28 December 1895, they were ready to show their invention to the public. The brothers opened the first cinema in the basement of the Grand Café in Paris. The films were very short and showed everyday subjects such as a crowd of workers coming out of a factory and a train pulling into a station. But the pictures moved, and the cinema had arrived!

By 1897, two years after the Lumières' first film show, no fewer than 358 short films had been made. By 1901, there were 1,299 films.

◀ The picture quality of early movies was very poor and, of course, they were in black and white. But the fact that the pictures moved was enough to attract viewers in their thousands.

Paperclip

It seems the simplest invention of all: a short length of bent wire that holds papers together. But the paperclip was redesigned many times before the version we use today was reached.

People used to hold their papers together with pins. But pins damaged the papers and could damage the user with a prick on the finger! One inventor who thought he could solve this problem was a Norwegian called Johan Vaaler. In 1901, he filed a patent for a wire paperclip. Several inventors came up with similar designs at around the same time.

There were problems with all these early paperclips. The end of the wire that stuck out as you pushed the clip down tended to stick in the paper and tear it, damaging the paper even more than a pin would have done. It was also difficult to make a machine to manufacture the clips. And obviously the cost of the labour involved in producing paperclips by hand would make the products too expensive.

The engineer William Middlebrook of Waterbury, Connecticut, solved the problem of the machine. He invented a machine for bending wire paperclips in 1899. It may also have been Middlebrook who came up with the answer to the other problem. For his machine made paperclips with a double loop, just like the ones we use today. These have become known as 'Gem' paperclips. They do not normally damage the paper.

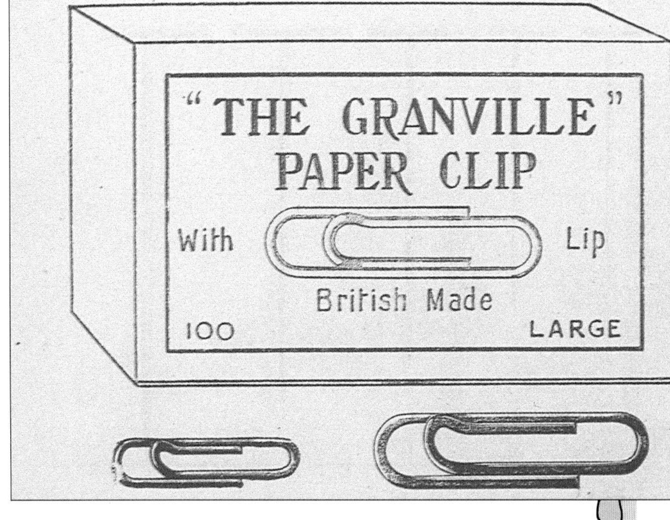

▲ The Granville paperclip is a variation on the classic double-looped design. It has what the manufacturers described as a 'lip'. The inner loop is bent upwards slightly, to help when pushing it on.

No one seems to have patented the Gem paperclip, so it is not certain who invented it. But it has become the standard design since it was introduced at the beginning of this century.

▼ Double-looped paperclips are now made with coatings of different-coloured plastic. As well as making the clips more attractive, users can 'code' their papers with different-coloured clips.

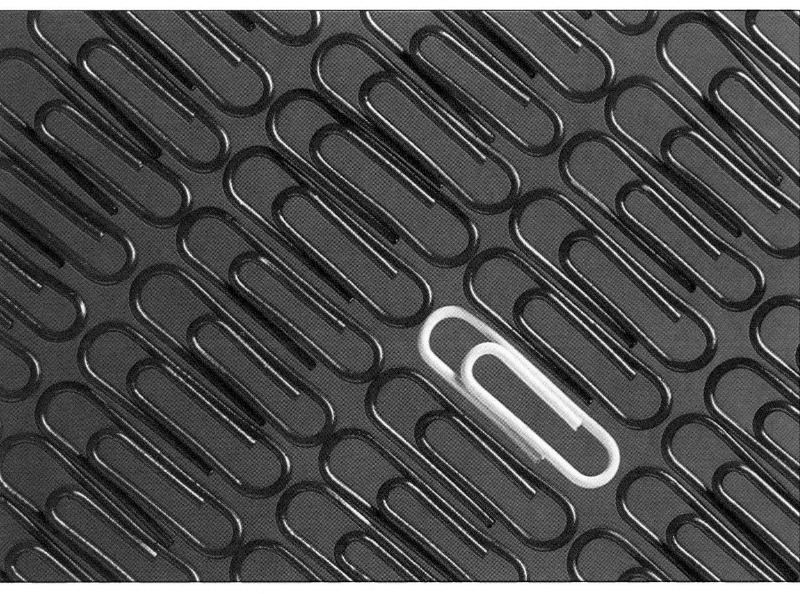

Vacuum cleaner

Several nineteenth-century inventors tried making a machine that would suck up dirt. Most machines used a bellows, which could be worked by hand. A number were made, including the successful 'Baby Daisy' model. But they were not labour saving – two people were needed to operate them, one to pump the bellows one to aim the nozzle.

British engineer Hubert Booth made the first effective vacuum cleaner in 1901. It had a petrol engine and was the first vacuum cleaner to have an efficient filter, a piece of fabric that kept the dirt in, but let the air back out into the room. It was a large, unwieldy device intended for use in factories. Booth's cleaners impressed American inventor J. Murray Spangler. In the 1900s, he made a smaller cleaner for home use and sold the rights to this design to a harness-maker called William H. Hoover. In 1908, Hoover started producing a small cleaner, which proved very popular. Since then, vacuum cleaners have been widely known as 'Hoovers'.

▲ The upright cleaner, with intake, dust-bag and handle in one unit, is one of the most popular types of vacuum cleaner. This one dates from 1952.

One nineteenth-century design for a vacuum cleaner was powered by a steam engine. Even for industrial use, this large machine stood little chance of catching on.

Radio

Guglielmo Marconi had invented radio by the time he was only 20 years old. After he read about the discovery of radio waves, he started to experiment in his parents' attic in Bologna. His genius was to bring together pieces of equipment that already existed and use them in new ways.

He had an electric spark generator, invented by Heinrich Hertz, the man who first detected radio waves in 1888. This he used as his transmitter. He also had a device called a 'coherer' that could turn radio waves into an electric current: this became the heart of his receiver.

When Marconi put these devices together in 1894, he found he could send radio waves across his attic and make them ring an electric bell connected to the coherer. Soon, he was experimenting with sending and receiving radio waves over much longer distances. In 1901, he even sent a radio signal across the Atlantic Ocean.

Marconi's work changed the world in all sorts of ways. Twenty years after his first Atlantic signal, millions of homes had radios to listen to. People in remote areas could use two-way radios to talk to one another. Ships could send radio signals when they were in distress. Radio has been entertaining us all and saving lives ever since.

▲ Guglielmo Marconi with his radio apparatus. He was still a young man when he worked out how to transmit and receive radio messages.

Marconi received little support for his invention at home in Italy, and he emigrated to England, where he built up a large business. In 1909, he shared the Nobel Prize for Physics with another radio pioneer, Karl Ferdinand Braun.

◀ In the early years of broadcasting, Marconi's company was a leading maker of radios for use in the home.

Lawn mower

Before the nineteenth century, people cut grass by hand, with a scythe. This was a laborious job, and required a lot of skill to get the grass short. A British engineer called Thomas Plucknett was the first to have the idea of making a machine to cut grass. He patented the first mowing machine in 1805. It was a cumbersome machine with a circular blade, and it did not work very well.

Other inventors saw Plucknett's machine and thought that they could do better. The most successful was Edwin Budding. He was an engineer in a textile factory and got the idea for his mower mechanism from one of the machines in the factory. His mower, made in 1830, was very similar to those used today. It was produced by several companies, including a firm called Ransome's of Ipswich. In 1899, Ransome's began to make motor mowers, powered by small petrol engines.

To cut grass effectively with a scythe, the grass has to be damp. With a lawn mower, on the other hand, it is best if the grass is dry. To begin with, people often kept a mower and a scythe, and chose which to use depending on the weather.

◀ Budding's machine was the first practical mower. It was very similar to cylinder hand mowers still in use today. As you pushed the handle, the mower moved and the blades turned. Clippings were thrown into the wooden box.

Hearing aid

Before the twentieth century, people with hearing difficulties had to rely on mechanical hearing aids. These often looked like metal trumpets. The owner put the narrow end to the ear and the speaker shouted into the wide end. Ear trumpets were some help, but it depended how bad your hearing was. They were also large and unwieldy. There was room for improvement.

One man who wanted to make a better hearing aid was Scottish inventor Alexander Graham Bell (see also pages 59 and 84). Bell worked out the principles of converting sound into an electrical signal that could be amplified. But his researches led him to invent not the hearing aid but the telephone.

It was left to another man, Miller Reese Hutchinson, to invent a usable electric hearing aid. His work at the end of the nineteenth century bore fruit in 1901, when his hearing aid was made. It was an instant success when used by the English queen Alexandra. She gave a medal to the inventor.

▲ In the 1920s, hearing aids were large, heavy and obvious, but they were a great improvement over the ear trumpets of the past.

King John VI of Portugal had an ear trumpet built into his throne in 1819. A kneeling servant could shout into a tube, which began in the arm of the throne and ended at the king's ear.

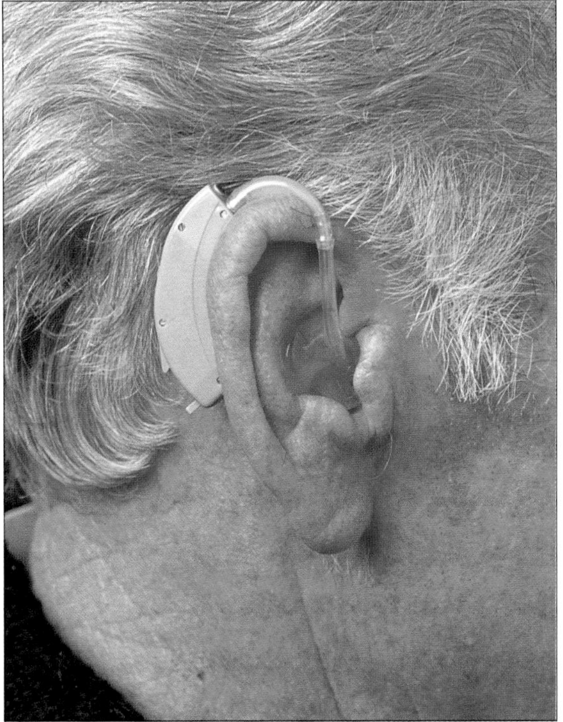

Unfortunately these early hearing aids were as large and cumbersome as the ear trumpets they were designed to replace. It was only in the 1920s that truly portable hearing aids were made, and even these weighed more than 2 lb (1 kg). Those with hearing difficulties had to wait until the invention of the transistor in the 1950s for small hearing aids, and for the arrival of the microprocessor (see page 105) in the 1970s for aids that could be worn, almost invisibly, in the ear.

◀ In this type of hearing aid, the microphone and amplifier are held in the unit that rests behind the ear, and a wire goes to a tiny in-ear speaker.

Aeroplane

It was 17 December 1903. Was today going to be the day? Wilbur and Orville Wright, bicycle manufacturers from Dayton, Ohio, had spent years working on their aircraft. Before them, many 'bird men' had tried and failed, making clumsy craft which failed to fly.

The Wrights' approach was different. They started with a simple kite with twin canvas wings on a wooden frame. They worked hard on it until it flew.

Next, they built a glider large enough to carry a pilot. Again, they modified it until it was safe. They trimmed the wings, and added a movable tail fin, so that the pilot could steer. The brothers travelled to the sand dunes at Kitty Hawk, North Carolina, to test their glider again and again. The work took all their spare time. Finally, after more than 1,000 glider flights, they were satisfied.

They fitted a powerful, lightweight petrol engine to the craft, now called *Flyer*, and tested it. On 17 December, with Orville at the controls, the first powered, controlled flight was made. In the following years, the Wrights made longer and longer flights, and paved the way towards worldwide air travel.

▲ In the years after the Wrights did their pioneering work, air travel gradually expanded. After World War I (1914–18), passenger services began to grow. Already the size of the world seemed to shrink with this new, fast form of transport. But with the appearance of the supersonic airliner Concorde in the 1960s, even faster travel became possible.

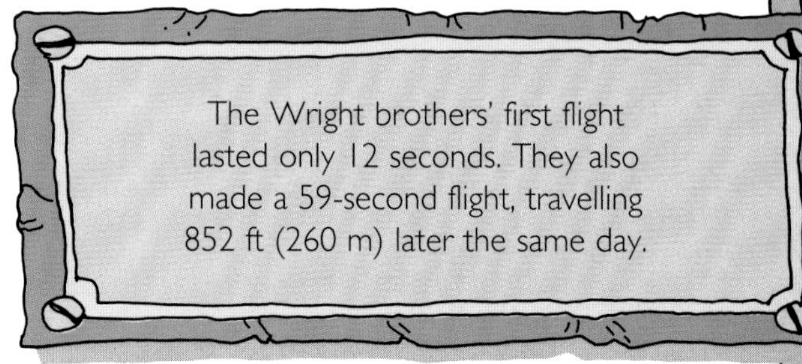
The Wright brothers' first flight lasted only 12 seconds. They also made a 59-second flight, travelling 852 ft (260 m) later the same day.

Frozen food

English seventeenth-century writer and philosopher Francis Bacon came to an untimely end after he caught a chill attempting to freeze a chicken by stuffing it with snow. Even before Bacon's unfortunate experiment, people knew that extreme cold would stop meat 'going bad', and this led to rich landowners setting up ice houses on their estates where food could be kept.

These early attempts at freezing food missed the important point. It is not so much the degree of cold as the speed with which the meat is frozen that is important. Probably the first person to realize this was the American inventor Clarence Birdseye. Birdseye was travelling in Labrador, carrying out a wildlife survey, in the years after World War I. He noticed that it was so cold that when he caught a fish, it quickly froze. He wondered whether this could be the key to food preservation.

Unlike Bacon, Birdseye lived in the age of the refrigerator. When he got home in 1923, he experimented using the refrigerator in his own kitchen. Then, Birdseye tried freezing different types of meat in a larger refrigeration plant.

Birdseye eventually found that the quickest way to freeze foods was to press the meat between a pair of refrigerated metal plates. By 1930, he was ready to start selling frozen foods from his factory at Springfield, Massachusetts.

▲ It was not until the 1950s and 1960s, when home refrigerators became common, that frozen foods began to sell in enormous quantities. Then Birdseye's famous red, white and blue packs became a familiar sight in shops in many parts of the world.

Frozen food soon became big business for Birdseye. Even before he invented his efficient twin-plate freezing process, his company was freezing up to 500 tonnes of fruit and vegetables a year.

▶ Thanks to Clarence Birdseye, frozen food is now a popular choice with many shoppers.

Washing machine

Today, it is difficult for most people in Europe and America to imagine life without a washing machine. But for thousands of years, people washed their clothes by hand. In many places, people still do their washing in the local river.

The first washing machine was worked by hand. It was a watertight box with a handle. The clothes and water were put in the box, and the handle was turned to move the clothes. By the 1880s, such machines were made with a built-in gas jet to heat the water.

But the first electric washing machine appeared in 1901. It was the brainchild of American Alva J. Fisher, and was like the hand-turned machines, except that the handle was replaced by an electric motor. This was a truly labour-saving design, but of course, it was only when mains electricity became common in homes that such machines were popular.

The makers of the first washing machines pointed out that the new machines were not only labour saving, but they were also kind to the clothes. One manufacturer claimed that sheets washed in his machine would last twice as long as those washed by hand.

▼ In this 1930s washing machine, the electric motor drove a rotor, which pushed the clothes around inside the tub.

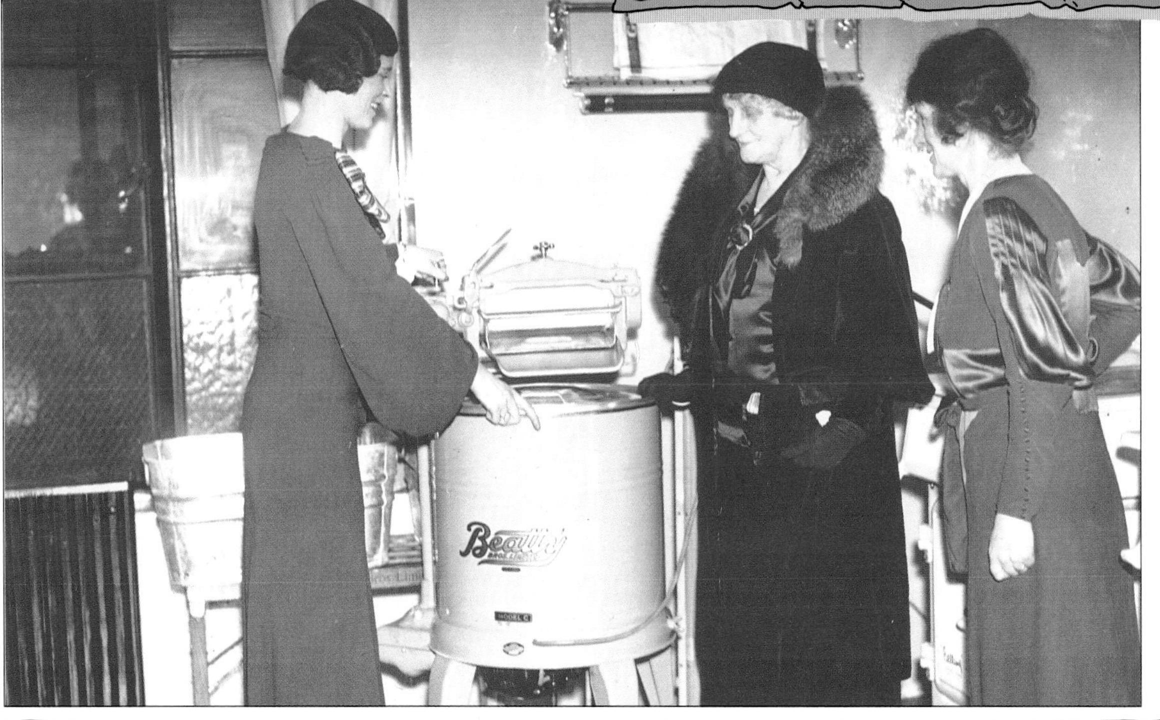

Fax

Sometimes an invention is made many years before there is any demand for it. This is what happened with the fax machine. The basic idea came to German inventor Arthur Korn in the early 1900s, but fax machines only became common in the 1980s. Korn invented a process called 'telephotography'. This enables any kind of image, either writing on a page, or an actual picture, to be broken up into a signal that can be sent on a wire and be 'redrawn' at the other end.

Korn's idea was taken up by a Frenchman, Edouard Belin, in the 1920s. In Belin's system, the image is scanned by a beam of light. The changes in the beam's intensity are picked up by a photoelectric cell and converted into electrical signals that can travel along a wire. The machine at the other end converts the signals back into an image.

Corporations such as RCA, Sharp and Rank Xerox developed Belin's system over the following decades.

The fax allows you to send someone an exact copy of your document. It takes its name from the word 'facsimile' from the Latin words *fac simile,* which mean 'make something like it'.

▲ Today, every office of any size has a fax machine that can send documents or pictures to any other fax machine in the world.

▶ Arthur Korn adjusts his machine for transmitting pictures, the ancestor of the fax.

Helicopter

People have always wanted to soar through the air like birds. Early on, inventors realized that one way to get lift was to use a spinning device called a 'rotor'. There is a sketch of this type of flying machine in the notebooks of Renaissance artist and inventor Leonardo da Vinci (see also page 46).

There was a lot of interest in 'rotorcraft', or helicopters as they became known, in nineteenth-century Europe. Brothers Louis and Jacques Breguet built an elaborate helicopter that had four rotors grouped around the pilot, who sat in the middle of the machine. The brothers tested their aircraft at Douai, France, in September 1907. They did not risk a free flight, but started the engine with the machine tethered to the ground by ropes. The helicopter rose about 1.5 metres (5 feet) before descending to the ground again.

Frenchman Paul Cornu was working on a helicopter at the same time. He made his first flight at Lisieux in November 1907. This time, the machine made a brief, low, untethered flight. Helicopters had got off the ground.

▲ The tail rotor is an important part of a helicopter. Without it, a single-rotor helicopter would spin in the air. The tail rotor is also used to steer the craft.

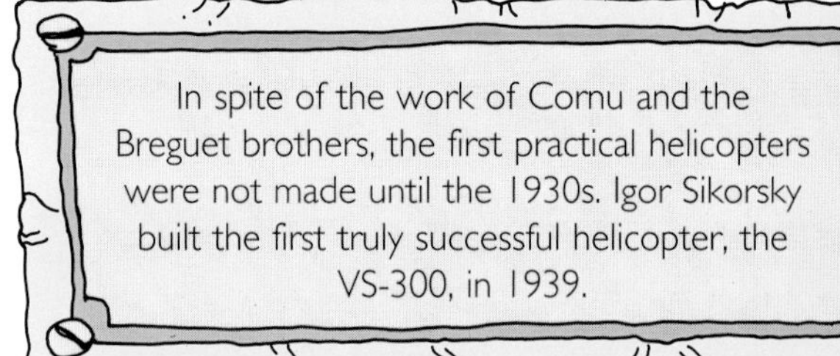
In spite of the work of Cornu and the Breguet brothers, the first practical helicopters were not made until the 1930s. Igor Sikorsky built the first truly successful helicopter, the VS-300, in 1939.

▼ Helicopters are now widely used by the military. Their ability to hover and land in confined spaces is valuable both in combat and when rescuing people trapped in otherwise inaccessible places.

Chemical fertilizers

Thousands of years ago, farmers realized that they could improve the soil with fertilizers. Early farmers put compost and animal manure on their soil. They knew that this worked, but they did not know why. The reason was that they were helping to replace nutrients, such as nitrogen, which are essential for plant growth.

Scientists in the nineteenth century discovered the importance of nitrogen. Farmers began to buy sodium nitrate, found naturally in deposits in Chile, to put on their fields. But these deposits would not last for ever, so they eventually needed to find another source of nitrogen. Fortunately, nitrogen is a common gas and makes up four-fifths of the Earth's atmosphere. So scientists began to look for ways of obtaining nitrogen from the atmosphere.

The man who succeeded was a German chemist called Fritz Haber. He devised a process of producing ammonia, which contains nitrogen, by reacting hydrogen and nitrogen with the help of a chemical catalyst (a substance that speeds up a reaction), perfected by chemist Carl Bosch. The process is now called the Haber-Bosch process. The process was made public in 1909 and the ammonia-production industry grew. Ammonia became the basis of chemical fertilizers and crop yields improved greatly.

▲ Chemical fertilizers have played a large part in feeding the world's growing population, especially in countries like India, where there has been a dramatic rise in the population. This Indian farmer uses a hand-pumped fertilizer spray.

The 'magic ingredients' in the Haber-Bosch process are the 'catalysts'. A catalyst is a substance that helps a chemical reaction take place without itself being changed. The catalysts in the Haber-Bosch process are nickel and iron.

◀ Bags of fertilizers are unloaded from a ship. Ecologists have criticized the use of chemical fertilizers, because of the possible contamination of the water supply. Also, large amounts of energy are used to produce the ammonia.

Hydrofoil

The hydrofoil reduces drag by lifting the hull of a boat out of the water. Unlike the hovercraft, which lifts its hull on a cushion of air, the hydrofoil's hull is raised on wings that skim across the water. When the boat is standing still, the wings are concealed underneath. But as the craft starts to move faster, the hull lifts out of the water.

The first boat that worked in this way was built by a Russian-born French nobleman, the Count de Lambert, in 1897. But little is known about it.

A year later, the Italian inventor Enrico Forlanini was working on the idea. Forlanini built his first hydrofoil in 1905. It could travel at a speed of 80 kph (50 mph), which was very fast for a boat at this time.

In 1911, Alexander Graham Bell (see also pages 59 and 77) came to Italy and saw one of Forlanini's hydrofoils on Lake Maggiore. Bell built his own hydrofoil, and other builders followed, although it was only in the 1950s that the craft were made in large numbers. Hydrofoils are still used in many places. They are especially suited to short-distance, high-speed sea travel.

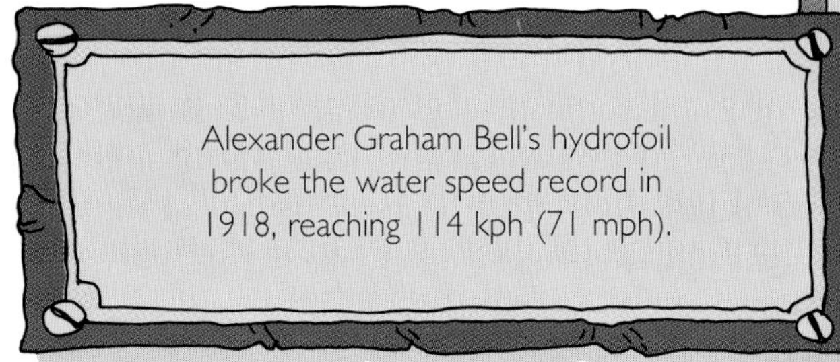

▼ The protruding foils push the hydrofoil's hull right out of the water. The result is less friction and more speed and efficiency. This hydrofoil rushes passengers from the Isle of Wight to the British mainland.

Combine harvester

Devices like the threshing machine (see page 40) and the mechanical reaper made farming much more efficient in the nineteenth century. It was possible to harvest more grain with fewer workers than ever before. But one late-nineteenth-century invention increased this efficiency still further. The combine harvester brings together the reaper and threshing machine in one unit. It allows the farmer to cut and thresh the corn in a single operation.

▲ The huge rotating framework on the front of a combine harvester pushes the tall standing corn towards the blades as it turns.

The first combine harvester was built by American inventor Hyram Moore in 1838. Combines became more common during the late 1880s in the USA, and similar machines soon followed in Australia.

There were several reasons why the combine harvester was taken up first in America and Australia. Farming is on a large scale in these countries. Fields can be huge, and a farmer with a quick method of harvesting can get the edge on his competitors. In addition, early combine harvesters were more suited to dry climates than damp ones. Before combines could be successful in Britain, drying machines had to be developed, because the cut corn was not dry enough to be stored straight away. Nowadays, the combine harvester is used all over the developed world.

Modern combine harvesters can harvest over 12 hectares (30 acres) of corn in a single day. At each pass across the field, they cut a swathe of corn about 5.5 m (18 ft) wide.

Stainless steel

One of the greatest discoveries of the nineteenth century was how to make steel. This metal is a mixture of iron and a controlled amount of carbon. It is easy to produce and very strong. Engineers used steel widely in the many new machines that were produced in the nineteenth century.

But there was one big problem with steel: it rusts easily. In tools that have to take a pounding and are exposed to moisture, it will corrode very quickly. As time went by, scientists tried to find a way around this by mixing other metals with the steel to make different rust-resistant alloys.

The most successful of these scientists was the British metallurgist Henry Brearley. In 1912, Brearley mixed chromium with steel to produce an alloy that was suitable for rifle barrels. He realized that the resulting metal was resistant to corrosion. Eventually he came up with a formula of 18 per cent chromium and 8 per cent nickel. Brearley suggested that this would be ideal for cutlery, and he had knives and forks made of the material in 1914. The metal became known as 'stainless steel'. It is now used for a vast range of goods.

▲ Stainless steel is very familiar in the kitchen. As well as cutlery, cookware, including pans, casseroles, steamers, and strainers, are all made of this metal. It is resistant to corrosion, easy to clean and conducts heat well, so it is an ideal material for these items.

There are more than a hundred different types of stainless steel in use today, with different percentages of chromium, nickel and other metals. All of these steels have special properties, such as the ability to be shaped easily when cold, or resistance to shock or corrosion.

◀ Stainless steel's rust-resistant quality, together with its gleaming appearance, made it popular for kitchen fittings in the mid-twentieth century. Sinks, hobs, door handles and even furniture were often made of stainless steel.

Detergents

Until the 1920s, most people did all their cleaning with soap. Soap is an efficient cleaner that can be made cheaply from readily available ingredients such as vegetable or animal fats. But it does have some drawbacks. It leaves a scum after use, and it can turn white items yellow.

People would probably have gone on using soap if it had not been for World War I. During this time, there was a shortage of fats in Germany as a result of a blockade by the Allies. Two chemists, called Gunther and Hetzer, who worked for one of the large German chemical companies, were given the job of finding an alternative. In 1917, they came up with the first synthetic detergent, which they called 'Nekal'. Until the end of the war, it proved a usable alternative to soap. But Nekal was not particularly effective as a detergent, and a lot of rubbing was needed before items would come clean.

In hard water, there are yet more problems with using soap as a detergent as it does not produce much lather. Synthetic detergents usually work much better.

IG Farben, the German company that marketed Nekal, continued research into detergents. So did the British firm Unilever. By 1929, chemists of Farben had worked out how to include fluorescent chemicals in soap powder. These chemicals reflect light as a bluish colour, producing a 'whiter-than-white' effect.

◀ Lux soapflakes, made by the British Unilever company, did not leave a scum and kept white clothes white, rather than turning them yellow.

Aerosol

The container of an aerosol contains two substances: the liquid that is to be sprayed and a propellant gas that is kept under pressure. When you press the button, a valve opens and the propellant forces out some of the liquid in a jet.

The first person to have this idea was the Norwegian scientist Erik Rotheim in 1926. But other inventors were also involved. American Julius S. Khan had the idea of the throw-away metal canister, and Lyle David Goodhue, also from the USA, developed the invention and made it marketable. The first aerosols went on sale in 1941.

Aerosols became widely used for a range of consumer products. Paints, cleaners, polishes, deodorants, perfumes, shaving cream and even whipped cream were widely sold in aerosols. They have also proved useful in health care, where they can be used for medicines for some lung diseases. But a problem with aerosols was discovered. The chemicals used for propellants were often chlorofluorocarbons (CFCs), substances that have proved damaging to the ozone layer in the Earth's upper atmosphere.

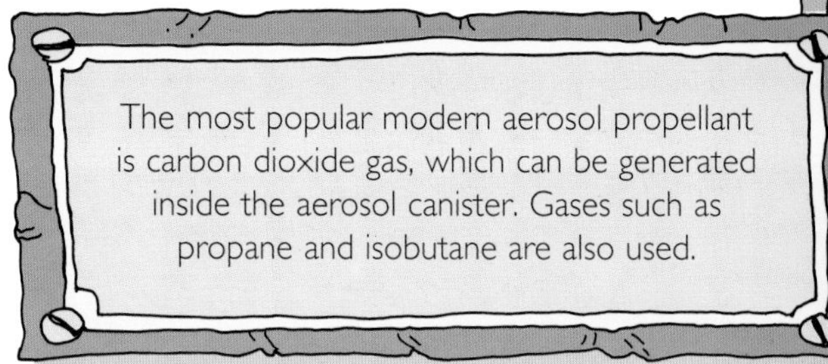
The most popular modern aerosol propellant is carbon dioxide gas, which can be generated inside the aerosol canister. Gases such as propane and isobutane are also used.

▼ In 1989, governments all over the world began to reduce the use of CFC propellants in aerosols. The chemicals have been banned in some countries. As a result, other propellants have been introduced.

Television

▲ John Logie Baird adjusts the scanner of his early mechanical television system.

The first television broadcasts began in London in 1929, using a system built by the flamboyant Scottish inventor John Logie Baird. The pictures caused a sensation, but they were nothing like modern television broadcasts. Today, colour television pictures are built up from 625 narrow lines; Baird's pictures had only thirty broad lines and were in black and white. This made the pictures very indistinct.

The reason Baird's pictures were so poor was that he used a primitive mechanical device to 'scan', or break down, the images. Baird argued very forcefully for his system, but other inventors were trying electronic devices that would do the same thing and produce much clearer pictures.

Many different engineers worked on electronic television systems. They included a British inventor called A. A. Campbell Swinton, and a Russian working in America, Vladimir Zworykin. All of their television systems had one thing in common, the device called the 'cathode ray tube' which produced the pictures. By the 1930s, the EMI company had started to develop the cathode ray tube. They created a television picture made up of 405 lines, a vast improvement on Baird's, which set the standard for many years.

▼ By the 1950s, television was becoming popular. Sets used the electronic system developed by EMI.

The latest development, high-definition television, promises pictures made up of over 1,000 scanning lines. These pictures will be sharper and clearer than any available on current televisions.

Sticky tape

If you bought a car in 1925, you wanted it to have the new fashionable two-tone paintwork. Unknown to most car-buyers, though, this fashion was causing problems for the workers who painted the cars. In order to stop the second colour covering the whole car, they had to cover part of the body with paper. But how could they make the paper stick to the car? Some adhesives were not strong enough, some were impossible to get off once the paint-job was finished.

It was a problem that was put to a young laboratory technician, Richard Drew, at the 3M company. He found that paint-workers had tried the surgical tape used in hospitals, but this tended to spoil the paintwork. He came up with a 2-inch-wide roll of crêpe paper coated with adhesive on one side. It worked perfectly. Soon, every car manufacturer was using his new masking tape.

But Drew did not leave it there. One day, he saw some clear cellophane in the lab. At the time, he was trying to find a way of making his tape waterproof, and he thought perhaps cellophane would be the material he needed. In fact, the cellophane tape was not waterproof. But it was clear and strong and made a sticky tape that was soon being used for all sorts of mending jobs. This sticky tape was soon to be found in every home.

'Masking tape', still available today, is similar to Drew's original tape for the car industry. Clear tape has been greatly improved since Drew's first cellophane tape, which yellowed and lost its stickiness with age.

◀ This French advertisement describes many uses for Scotch tape – such as mending books, fixing labels and making models.

Tape recording

The first ‘tape recorders’ did not use tape at all, but lengths of steel piano wire. They worked in the same way as the modern tape recorder, though. The steel wire recorder was the idea of Valdemar Poulsen, an engineer who worked for the Copenhagen Telephone Company. He invented a way of magnetizing the piano wire in response to an incoming sound from a microphone. The sound was ‘stored’ on the wire in the form of tiny magnetized areas. Poulsen’s machine, designed in 1898, was called the ‘telegraphone’.

Poulsen’s patent application also included details of a machine that would use a paper tape coated with metallic powder. This was the first tape recorder, but it was never manufactured.

Few people saw the importance of Poulsen’s invention. Only a few telegraphones were ever produced in the USA, mainly for dictation and recording telephone messages.

▲ Small tape recorders soon caught on in the office, where they could be used for dictating letters – and even recording telephone conversations.

In the 1930s, the invention was revived by two firms in Germany, Farben and Telefunken. Their engineers used a plastic tape coated with iron oxide, but otherwise the machine worked in the same way as Poulsen’s machine. A pattern of magnetization was left on the tape from the amplified signal from the microphone, and the tape was wound on to large round reels. Soon tape recorders were being used widely for professional recording.

Early reel recorders were large, costly and fiddly to use. In the 1960s, Philips introduced the compact cassette, in which the tape is contained ready-wound in a small plastic box. With this much simpler system, tape recorders became common in the home.

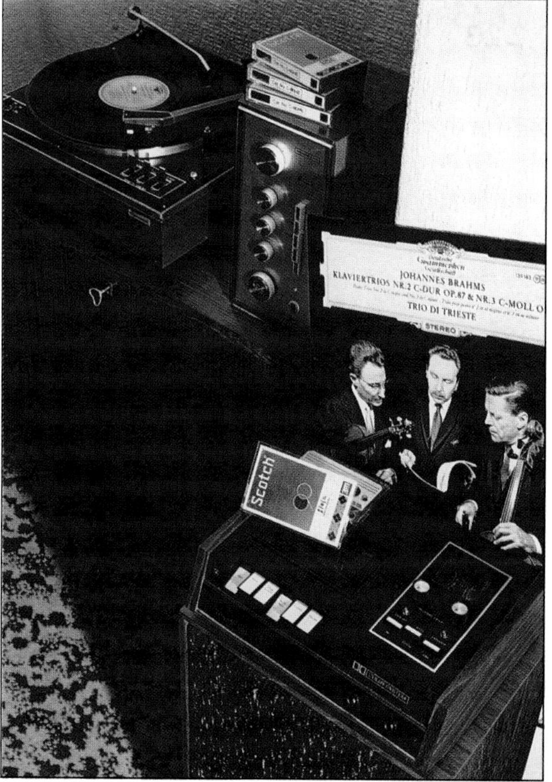

◀ When the compact cassette was established, hi-fi manufacturers began to produce cassette tape decks that could be hooked up to a stereo system to give sound of very high quality.

Jet engine

We take for granted fast, regular flights connecting all the world's major cities. Much of this efficient air travel is powered by the jet engine, which was developed during World War II.

The jet engine works because, in nature, every action has an equal and opposite *re*action. Fuel is burned in the heart of the engine, exhaust gases stream out of the back, and so the engine moves forwards.

Two men realized that this method could be used to power aircraft. British engineer Frank Whittle published the principle in 1928. But working independently, German inventor Hans Ohain patented a design based on the idea in 1930.

During World War II, the work of Whittle and Ohain carried on, still independently, of course, because Britain and Germany were at war. It seemed that there would be a huge military advantage to whichever country came up with a jet-powered aircraft that could be manufactured quickly. In the event, the Germans produced the first jet aircraft to fly, the Heinkel He-178 of 1939. The British followed in 1941 with the Gloster E-28.

Both aircraft needed further work, and it was only towards the end of the war that jet aircraft went into regular production. So it was in the years after the war that jet aircraft began to take over in the skies.

▲ Frank Whittle (right) points out the details of a model of an early jet engine.

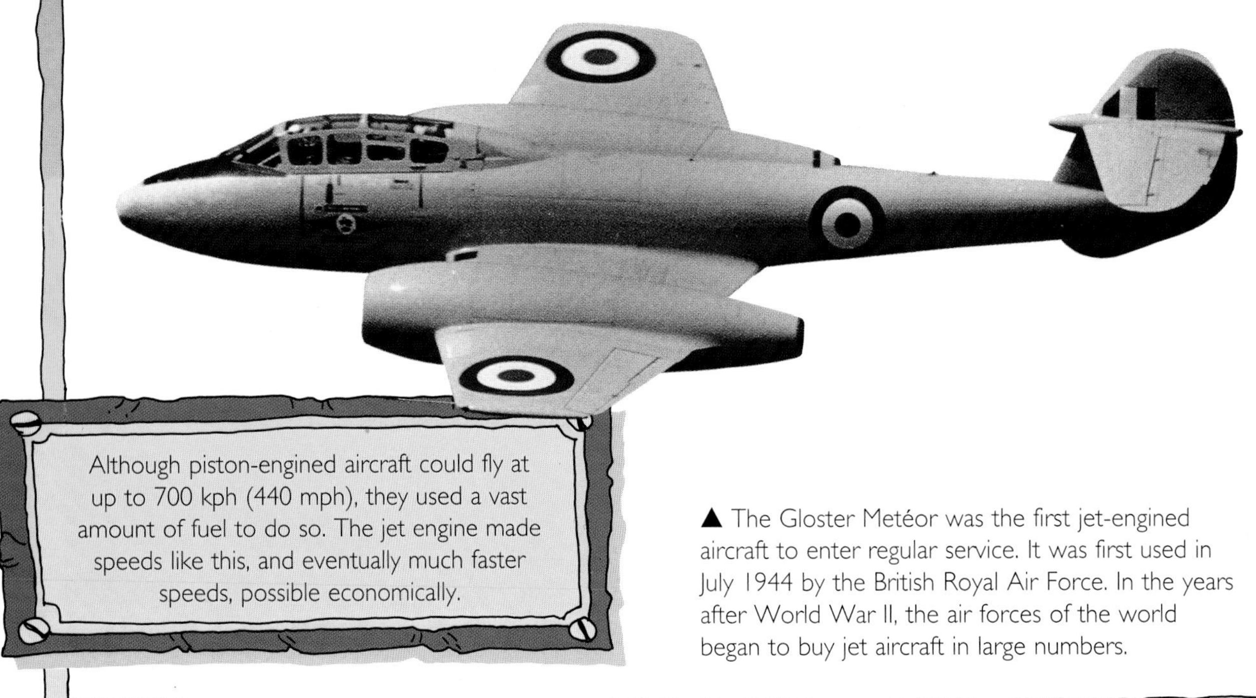

▲ The Gloster Metéor was the first jet-engined aircraft to enter regular service. It was first used in July 1944 by the British Royal Air Force. In the years after World War II, the air forces of the world began to buy jet aircraft in large numbers.

Although piston-engined aircraft could fly at up to 700 kph (440 mph), they used a vast amount of fuel to do so. The jet engine made speeds like this, and eventually much faster speeds, possible economically.

Parking meter

The USA was the first place in the world where the car became vital to everyday life. Huge numbers of vehicles were on the road by 1930. In the vast spaces of the open country, this was fine. But there were problems of crowding in the cities. People often found it impossible to find a parking space. One man who was especially aware of this was a journalist, Carlton C. Magee. He worked on the *Oklahoma City Newspaper* and was also president of the local Businessmen's Traffic Committee.

Magee realized that one way to make the situation fairer would be to make people pay for a set amount of parking time. So he developed the parking meter. Inserting a coin allowed the motorist to turn a knob, which controlled a needle display showing how much time had passed since the knob was turned. Once the needle had returned to its original position, the parking time was up.

Magee's original parking meters were unwieldy devices that looked like loaves of bread on posts. Three years after his original patent, Magee had modified the design to a wedge-shape, which is very similar to the parking meters of today.

▼ Parking meters are a familiar sight in many cities today. They allow motorists to park on the street for a limited time, and so help to keep traffic moving.

Instant coffee

Coffee is native to Ethiopia. It was used as a drink in northern Africa and western Asia for hundreds of years before it arrived in Europe in the seventeenth century. Plantations were set up in hot, moist climates all over the world, and coffee became a popular drink. But it takes a lot of effort to make a good pot of coffee. The beans have to be ground into a fine powder. It is also best to use some sort of filter to keep the grounds out of the cup, although people in many places enjoy drinking unfiltered coffee.

All this effort inspired inventors to look for an easier way of making a cup of coffee. Although there were several attempts in the nineteenth century, none was successful. Then in 1930, the Brazilian Institute of Coffee approached the Swiss company Nestlé, asking them to try to produce a form of dried coffee that would produce an instant drink when it was mixed with hot water.

Nestlé spent eight years on the research. They found that the most effective way was to spray concentrated coffee extract through a jet of hot air. The heat evaporated the water in the coffee extract, leaving particles of dried coffee. This powder would dissolve easily in boiling water to produce an acceptable drink. The new instant coffee was marketed under the name of Nescafé, a brand that has been famous around the world ever since.

Nowadays, a freeze-drying process is also used to make instant coffee. This involves freezing the coffee and then vapourizing its water content. The process was invented in 1906, but was only widely used in the last few decades. Manufacturers claim that this method preserves more of the original flavour.

◀ Travellers to the city of Damascus in the sixteenth century enjoy cups of coffee made from beans roasted over an open fire. It would be hundreds of years before coffee would become a truly popular drink in the West. With the arrival of Nescafé, coffee became still more widespread in Europe and the USA.

Ballpoint pen

Before the invention of the ballpoint pen, writing could be a messy business. Simple steel-nibbed pens, which you had to keep dipping into a pot of ink, were used in both schools and offices. It was easy to upset the ink pot and even easier to blot or smudge your work.

One man who was fed up with the old dip pens was a Hungarian journalist and proof-reader called Laszlo Biro. He and his colleagues were always complaining about blots and smudges, so when Biro saw some quick-drying ink in a paint shop in the late 1930s, he decided to try to do something about it.

It took Laszlo and his brother Georg, who was a chemist, several years of experimenting before they came up with their design. It was a tube filled with quick-drying ink, tipped with a ball bearing, which delivered the ink smoothly to the paper.

By the time they had perfected their idea, the brothers had emigrated to Argentina, where they found a backer in English businessman Henry Martin. By 1943, they were making ballpoint pens and selling them to the English military and RAF. During the post-war years, cheaper manufacturing methods were developed, and the ballpoint pen became everyone's favourite writing tool.

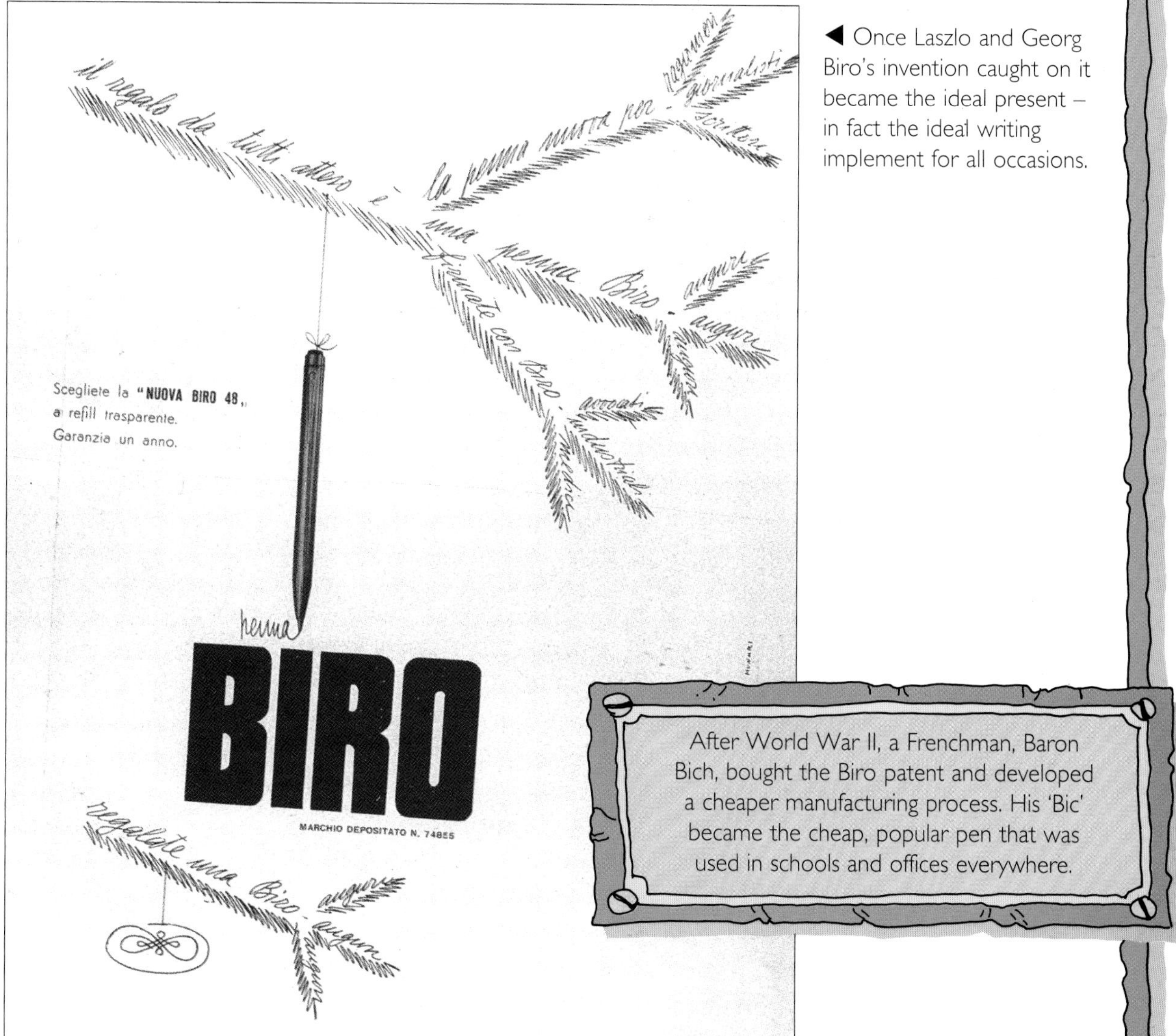

◀ Once Laszlo and Georg Biro's invention caught on it became the ideal present – in fact the ideal writing implement for all occasions.

After World War II, a Frenchman, Baron Bich, bought the Biro patent and developed a cheaper manufacturing process. His 'Bic' became the cheap, popular pen that was used in schools and offices everywhere.

Microwave oven

In 1940, two British inventors, John Randall and H. A. Boot, devised a piece of equipment called a 'magnetron'. This produces microwave energy, a type of short-wave radiation. Its first use was to improve radar systems in World War II.

Percy Le Baron Spencer was a physicist who worked for Raytheon, a maker of radar equipment. When using a magnetron, Spencer noticed that the radiation produced by the magnetron in turn produced heat. Spencer began to wonder how he could harness this heat. He was soon melting chocolate and popping corn with his magnetron.

Microwaves make the molecules in food vibrate, so that the food heats up. The process happens very quickly, even though the waves do not heat up anything made of paper, china or glass. This makes microwaving a very convenient form of cooking. The short cooking times also save energy.

In 1945, a purpose-made microwave oven was produced, but it was a long time before microwave ovens were successful in the domestic market.

▲ This early microwave cooker was too large for most kitchens. It was a long time before units small and cheap enough for the home were produced. When they were, they were soon popular.

Simple foods cook best in a microwave. If a food is a mixture of liquid and dry substances, microwave cooking does not work so well, because the liquids cook faster than the drier parts.

Computer

The first electronic computers were a far cry from the powerful desktop machines of today. They weighed tonnes, and had a memory capacity of just a few numbers and letters. One of the first such machines was developed in America by a team of scientists led by John Mauchly and John Eckert. They built it between 1942 and 1946, and called it ENIAC, the Electronic Numerical Integrator and Computer.

ENIAC's tiny memory meant that it was very difficult to use. It was also very unreliable, because it contained around 18,000 valves, which tended to overheat and often needed replacing. But it was a start. ENIAC could add two numbers in 0.2 milliseconds, meaning that it could do in one day calculations that would take a human mathematician a year.

Later developments of the computer began by making it easier to use. 'Programs', or series of instructions telling the computer what to do, were written; ways were found of increasing computer memories; and devices such as keyboards were added, making it easier to input the data required.

▲ The first computers were very difficult to use. Modern machines are designed to be so simple that the youngest children can operate them!

Perhaps the greatest leap forward came with the invention of the transistor (see page 100) in 1947. This provided a smaller replacement for the valve, and one which did not heat up. Suddenly, computers became smaller and more reliable, and the modern 'information age' had truly begun.

◀ John Mauchly at the controls of ENIAC. Numbers had to be entered using hundreds of dials – the process was laborious compared with today's keyboards, but revolutionary at the time.

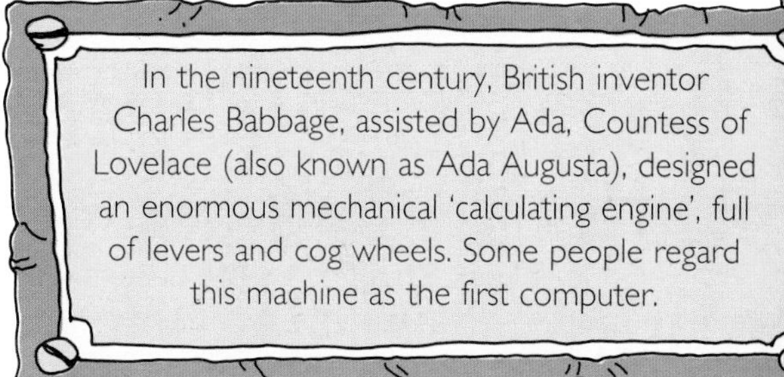

In the nineteenth century, British inventor Charles Babbage, assisted by Ada, Countess of Lovelace (also known as Ada Augusta), designed an enormous mechanical 'calculating engine', full of levers and cog wheels. Some people regard this machine as the first computer.

Chemical pesticides

Anyone who grows plants knows the problems caused by pests, especially insects that eat away leaves and fruit. Since the time of the ancient Greeks and Romans, farmers have tried to combat insect pests with pesticides. In the twentieth century, scientists searched for a truly powerful pesticide that could be used in large-scale agriculture.

A breakthrough came in 1939, when the Swiss scientist Paul Müller discovered that a chemical called DDT (dichloro-diphenyl-trichloro-ethane) is a powerful insecticide. DDT was used in Switzerland against the Colorado potato beetle. It was also used to wipe out malaria-carrying mosquitoes. During World War II, DDT also proved useful in protecting troops against diseases carried by insects.

DDT is a strong, long-lasting poison, but insects gradually developed a resistance to it, and doses had to be doubled in the 1950s. This meant that the chemical also posed a danger to humans. Many Western countries have now banned DDT, but it is still used elsewhere, for example, against malarial insects, where the advantages to human health outweigh the drawbacks.

The experience with DDT showed that chemical pesticides, although powerful, can be dangerous as they can enter the food chain. Fields were routinely sprayed in the 1950s and 1960s, but farmers are now much more careful about the chemicals they use.

▲ This tractor is fitted with a spraying device that was designed to eliminate Colorado beetles from European potato crops.

Today, many gardeners are returning to 'natural', plant-derived chemicals like pyrethrum, which comes from chrysanthemum flowers, to kill insects.

◀ Crop spraying with aeroplanes and helicopters was common in the 1960s but is much less widespread now.

Record (LP)

In the early years of this century, sound recordings were made on cylinders and later discs made of hard materials like shellac. They were played with a heavy steel needle, which produced poor sound quality. Each side lasted for only a few minutes.

American engineers H. C. Harrison and H. A. Frederick were working on the problem in 1931. They realized that if a softer material was used for the disc, and if this was reproduced with a lighter needle, sound quality would be improved. But the time was not right for their ideas. People were still suffering from the poverty that came after the Wall Street stock market crash of 1929. The last thing they wanted to spend their money on was new records. The work of Harrison and Frederick was forgotten, and people continued to listen to their old 78 rpm (revolutions per minute) discs.

Another American, Peter Goldmark, who worked for Columbia, picked up the idea in the 1940s. Developments in record players now meant that a tiny stylus could replace the old metal needles. So Goldmark was able to design a record with very narrow grooves, which would sound much better and play for much longer, than the old discs. The new 33.3 rpm discs could hold about twenty-five minutes per side, so, not surprisingly, they became known as 'long-playing records' or LPs. However, today's CDs (see page 107) are able to hold even more music.

▲ With the arrival of long-playing records, many different tracks could be included on the same disc, making more music available in smaller packages.

The 78 rpm discs of the 1920s and 1930s had about eighty grooves per inch, while LPs have up to 250 grooves per inch. It was this larger number of microscopic grooves that enabled manufacturers to cram about twenty-five minutes of music on each side.

◀ These labels from old 78 rpm records show how little music could be included on a single side – only part of a single movement of a classical symphony, for example.

Transistor

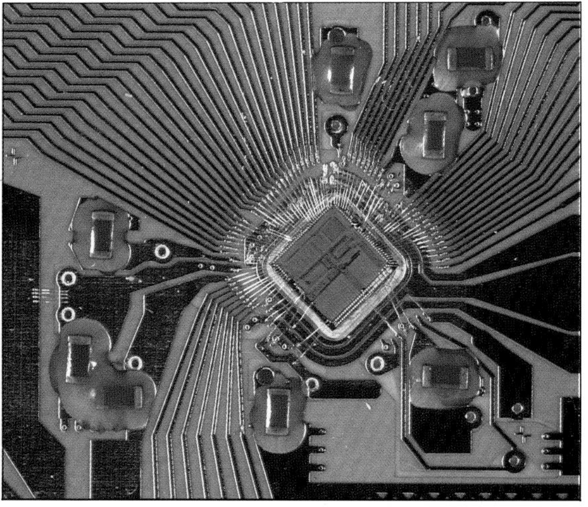

▲ Transistors today are made so small that they are invisible to the human eye. 450,000 transistors are included on this tiny microchip.

Early electronic equipment was cumbersome and unreliable. Computers were the size of large rooms, television sets were huge pieces of furniture with tiny screens. The main reason for this was that they were full of devices called 'valves', which were vacuum tubes used to amplify the electric current or turn it on and off. Computers needed thousands of these devices, a radio receiver had a handful. Valves also heated up, so devices like radios and televisions had to have plenty of space for air to circulate inside the cabinet. A final problem with valves was that their life was short, so they needed replacing regularly, like light bulbs.

In 1947, a group of scientists, John Bardeen, Walter Brattain and William Shockley, working at the Bell Laboratories in the USA came up with an alternative: the transistor. Transistors are small, reliable, and do not get hot. They are simple devices made of layers of semiconducting materials such as silicon that affect the current passing through them. Transistors are efficient amplifiers of current, making them ideal in devices like televisions, hi-fi components, hearing aids, radios, and other appliances in which signals have to be made louder. They can also be used as switches, hence their usefulness in computers, which consist of thousands of switches. Transistors have made possible the dozens of small, reliable electronic appliances that can be seen in every home and office.

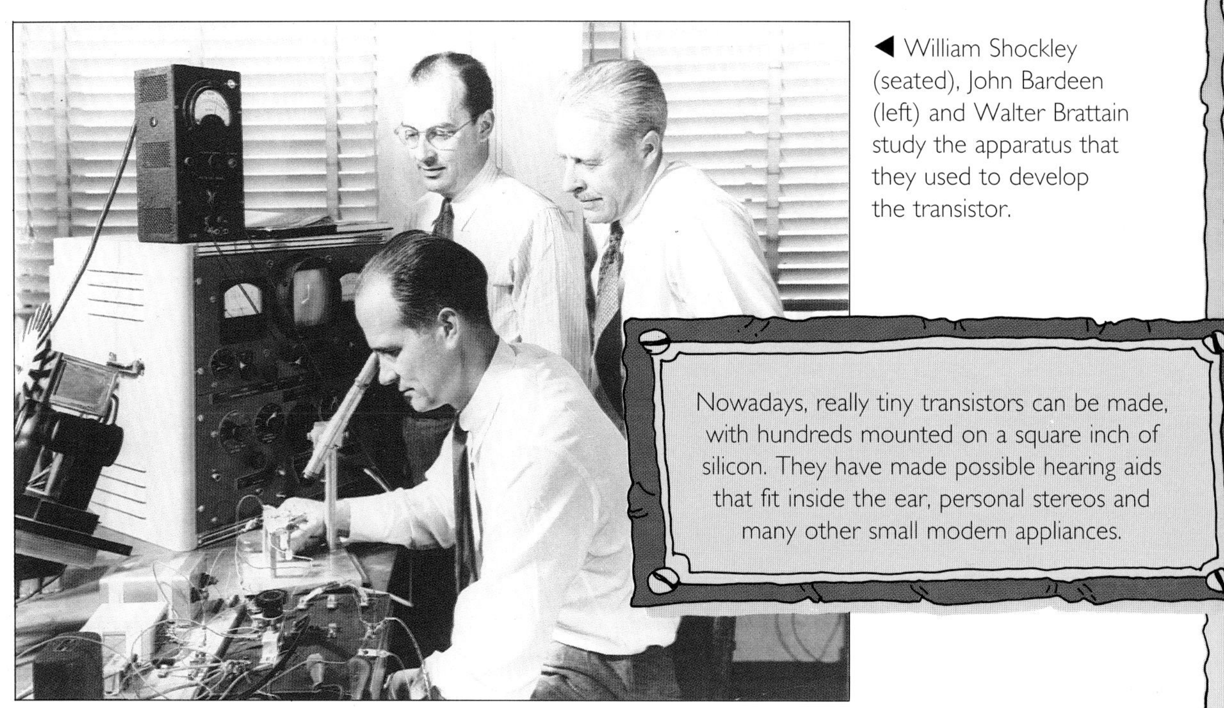

◀ William Shockley (seated), John Bardeen (left) and Walter Brattain study the apparatus that they used to develop the transistor.

Nowadays, really tiny transistors can be made, with hundreds mounted on a square inch of silicon. They have made possible hearing aids that fit inside the ear, personal stereos and many other small modern appliances.

Credit card

▲ Credit card symbols are so well known today that they form a sort of international language. Banks all over the world display the cards that they accept.

The first credit cards were issued in the 1920s. Several American oil companies had the idea of issuing cards that allowed customers to buy petrol on credit and pay the bill later. It was a simple and effective idea, but it did not catch on until much later. Another early credit card was the Diners' Club card, issued by Ralph Schneider in New York in 1950. It allowed members to eat at twenty-seven New York restaurants.

To begin with, these credit cards could only be used in a small number of outlets. But Schneider soon had the idea of extending the validity of his card to shops as well as restaurants. Soon the idea of the 'universal' card, valid almost anywhere, came into being. In 1958, the first bank card, the Bankamericard of the Bank of America, was introduced.

Another important invention, the computer, made this change possible. By the mid-1950s, computers were being used in businesses for the first time, meaning that information about customers' accounts could be gathered in one place and stored easily. Since then, other innovations have made credit cards more secure and easier to use. One example is the idea of adding a magnetic strip to the card, on which information about the owner's identity, or a personal identification number (PIN), can be recorded.

◀ A range of familiar credit cards. Nowadays cards like these are used for a variety of purposes – to obtain cash advances at a bank, to guarantee cheques, and of course to buy goods on credit as was originally intended.

Cards with a built-in microchip on which details of the holder's bank account and other information can be stored, are growing in popularity. These are known as 'smart cards'.

Non-stick pan

The non-stick pan is a good example of an invention that came about by accident, in fact by two accidents.

The first accident was in 1938. Roy J. Plunkett was working for the Du Pont company in the USA as a researcher into refrigerant chemicals, but in the course of this he accidentally came across the chemical polytetrafluoroethylene, or PTFE. Useless as a refrigerant, PTFE has other useful qualities. It resists attack by other chemicals, it will withstand high temperatures and it has low-friction properties.

The second accident came about in 1954, because another engineer, Frenchman Marc Grégoire, was a keen fisherman. He knew about PTFE and its low-friction properties, and decided to use some to stop his fishing line sticking. His wife said he should try to stop the food from sticking to her kitchen pans, and Grégoire realized that PTFE would do this too. Two years later, Grégoire founded the Tefal company to produce pans coated with PTFE. Grégoire also realized that no one would remember the name of his chemical coating, and so gave it a new name, 'Teflon®'.

▲ Many foods stick to an ordinary metal pan when they are fried. Teflon, with its low-friction properties, stops the food sticking.

PTFE is now used widely on many items where a non-stick surface is useful. Examples include skis and many pieces of laboratory equipment. It is also used for wire insulation, partly because of its resistance to high temperatures.

▼ Well-known television cook Philip Harben launched his own brand of non-stick cookware in the 1960s. It was one of several successful brands.

Video recording

To begin with, all television broadcasts were 'live'. There was no method of storing pictures for later broadcast, let alone any way of recording them in the home. In the 1950s, the Ampex Company began to produce machines that would record pictures on magnetic tape. The tape was similar to that used for sound recording, but at 2 ins (5 cm) across was much wider. Ampex machines were large, expensive, and designed for use by television stations.

The Japanese Sony corporation were the first to produce a video recorder for use in the home. It was not a cassette recorder, but used large reels of tape. Large and expensive, it was not a commercial success. But the breakthrough came with the video cassette recorder (VCR), which was introduced by Philips in the early 1970s. This was cheaper, more compact, and much easier to use than earlier machines.

For a while, there was no single standard for the size of video cassettes, and three different systems were produced, all incompatible with each other. Eventually two of the three formats went out of production, leaving the video home system (VHS), which was introduced in 1975 by the Japanese company JVC, with the lion's share of the market.

Video discs, using the same technology as the compact disc (see page 107) to reproduce television pictures, are now available, but because of the convenience of video tape for home recording, they have been slow to catch on.

▼ Modern video recorders are designed to be easy to use, with a remote control unit and a microprocessor that makes programming simple.

Photocopier

Few inventions have transformed office life as much as 'Xerography'. Before photocopiers came on to the market, if you wanted a copy of a document you had three alternatives: copy it out on a typewriter or by hand, have it photographed, or take it to a printer. The first was long-winded, the second and third costly and the third also useless if you only wanted a single copy.

American physicist Chester Carlson worked on the answer to this problem in the 1930s. He devised a process in which an electrostatic charge is induced on a surface. Light from the original is reflected on to the surface, which varies the charge. When the 'toner', a coloured dust, is charged and blown over the surface, it is attracted to the pattern of the image but rejected by the background, resulting in a copy.

Carlson filed a patent for a copying machine in 1939. But it was over ten years before the copier was marketed.

▲ Chester Carlson with his first photocopier. The design was eventually taken up by the Haloid company, who changed its name to Xerox. The first copier was launched in 1950.

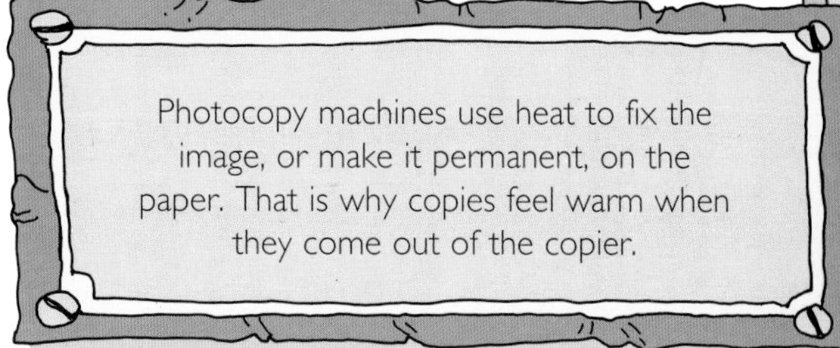

Photocopy machines use heat to fix the image, or make it permanent, on the paper. That is why copies feel warm when they come out of the copier.

◀ Modern office copiers are highly versatile. They can photocopy on to different paper sizes, enlarge the image, and some even copy in colour.

Microprocessor

At the heart of every computer is a small circuit called a 'microprocessor'. It forms the computer's central processing unit, the part of the machine that controls the flow of data and performs instructions in response to whatever program the computer is running.

The microprocessor is an 'integrated circuit', which means that it is contained on a single piece, or 'chip', of silicon, and is made as a single unit. It is both very small and very powerful.

The first microprocessor was made in 1972. It was designed by Marcian E. Hoff, who worked for Intel, a company that still makes large numbers of microprocessors for the computer industry. This original processor carried the equivalent of 230 transistors.

Since Hoff's first processor, microprocessors have increased in their sophistication and speed. Modern 32-bit processors are able to carry out more than four million instructions per second. Faster processors allow more complex programs to be run.

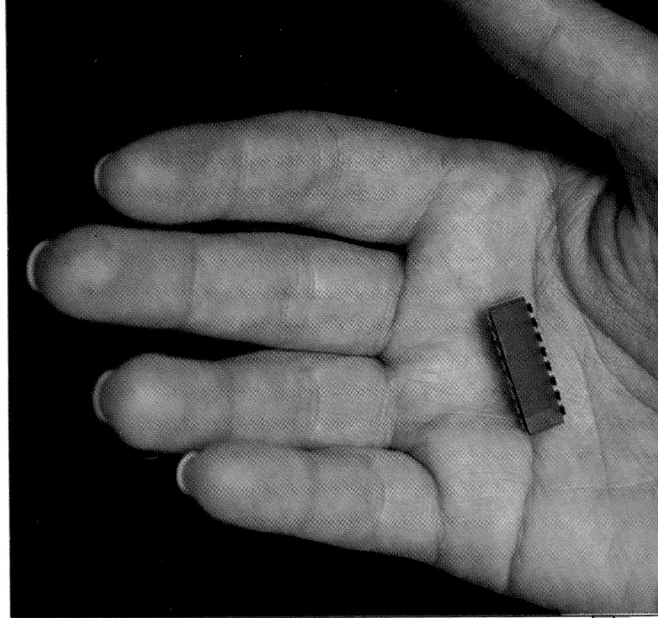

▲ The microprocessor, or integrated circuit, is very small but it allows the computer to run very complex programs.

One of the most demanding functions of a modern computer is controlling the display, which nowadays is usually in colour and capable of displaying detail in high resolution. This is why computer manufacturers often include a special extra microprocessor, just to control the graphics.

◀ Microprocessors are used wherever machines need some form of automatic control. All modern office machines, including these portable devices, contain microprocessors. So do washing machines, video recorders and televisions.

Electronic calculator

At school, we all have to master the basics of arithmetic. Everyone has to learn how to add, subtract, multiply, and divide – but everyone longs to get to the point where they are allowed to use a pocket calculator to do all but the simplest sums.

Once you have used a calculator, it is hard to manage without one. And yet the first electronic pocket calculator was only produced in 1972. It was designed by a team of scientists who worked for the American company Texas Instruments. To begin with, pocket calculators were costly items of equipment. But they soon came down in price and now almost everyone has one – to work out everything from the weekly shopping bill to complex mathematical theorems.

Modern calculators can be as small as credit cards – and the only thing that prevents them getting even smaller is that the keys have to be large enough for human fingers to operate. Many have a small memory in which figures can be stored. Soon after the appearance of the first electronic calculator,, manufacturers started to produce specialist models to suit particular needs.

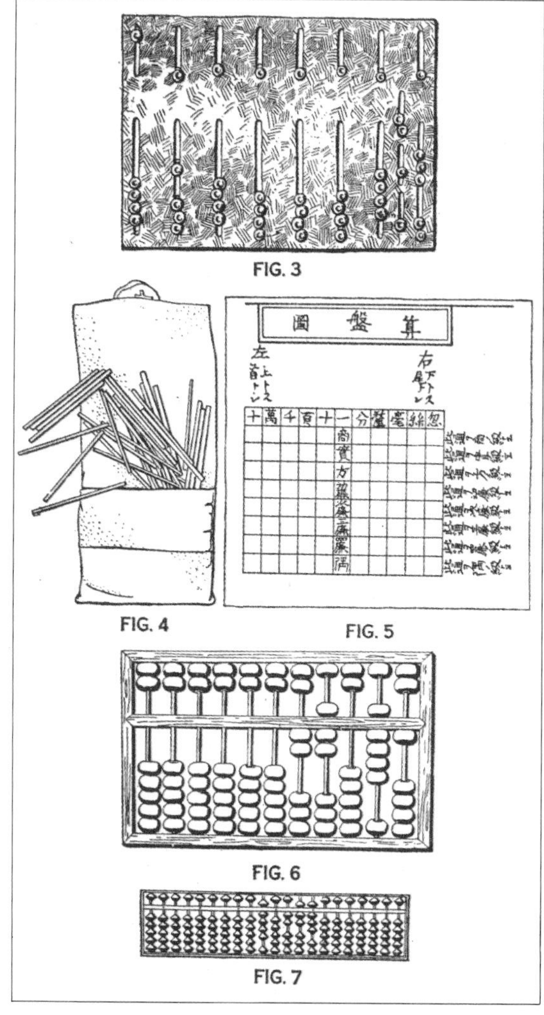

▲ The abacus, with its moving beads, is still a popular calculating aid in the Far East. This engraving shows a Roman abacus (top) and abacuses from China, Japan and Korea.

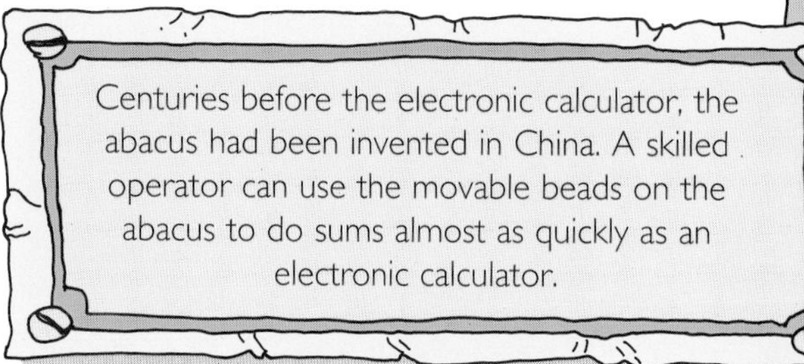

Centuries before the electronic calculator, the abacus had been invented in China. A skilled operator can use the movable beads on the abacus to do sums almost as quickly as an electronic calculator.

◀ Calculators have a floating-point display, which means that the position of the decimal point can move, enabling a wide range of different values to be worked out. This calculator is powered by a small solar cell, so it does not even need batteries.

Compact disc

Vinyl LPs (see page 99) brought music into almost every home. They were easy to make and, with the right equipment, could produce superb sound. But there were many problems with LPs. They could be scratched easily, resulting in irritating clicks, the sound was distorted easily if the turntable did not revolve at an even speed, and a speck of dust could create a crackle.

In the late 1970s, the Dutch Philips company and the Japanese Sony corporation worked together to come up with an alternative: the compact disc (CD). CDs store the music in the form of a series of pits and plateaux on their surface. These make up a type of digital computer code. In the CD player, they are scanned by a laser beam and translated back into music.

When the first CDs and CD players came out in 1979, people were amazed.

▲ The gleaming surface of a CD is in fact made up of millions of microscopic pits, which carry the music in the form of a digital code.

The lack of noise from dust or scratches gives a 'clean' sound, far better than that produced by LPs to most peoples' ears. CDs are much less vulnerable to wear and tear than LPs. In addition, up to 110 minutes of music could be fitted on a single disc.

Finally, CDs are much easier to use than LPs. Because they are computer controlled, any track on the CD can be selected instantly, individual tracks can be repeated at the touch of a button, or selected in any order.

◀ People usually buy a CD player as part of a complete sound system, which allows them to play music from a range of different sources. This system contains (from top to bottom): CD player, twin cassette deck, radio tuner and amplifier.

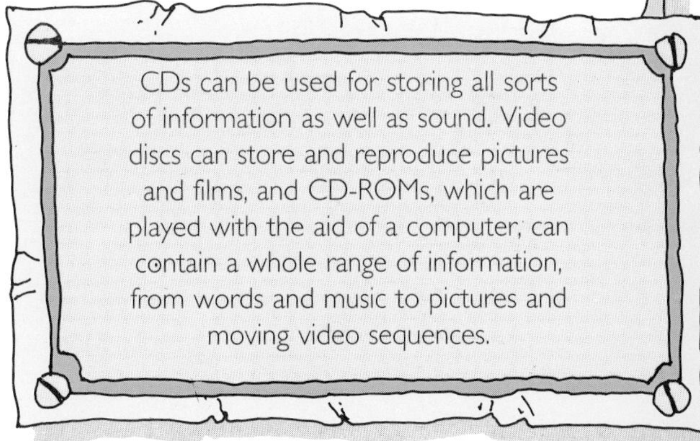

CDs can be used for storing all sorts of information as well as sound. Video discs can store and reproduce pictures and films, and CD-ROMs, which are played with the aid of a computer, can contain a whole range of information, from words and music to pictures and moving video sequences.

Jumbled Alphabet Acrostic

Unscramble the letters to solve the questions.

The 'source' column tells you where to find the answers.

clues		source
Company that produced machines to record pictures on magnetic tape	XPAEM	Video recording
Designer of the first vacuum cleaner	HTBOO	Vacuum cleaner
Means of lifting an elevator cage	LACEB	Elevator
Machine that sows seeds evenly	LIRLD	Seed drill
Designer of the first practical lawn mower (first name)	WENDI	Lawn mower
First to extract nitrogen from the atmosphere (first name)	ZRFTI	Chemical fertilizers
Light bulbs are made of this	SLGAS	Electric light bulb
Developer of early plastics	THYTA	Plastics
Material first used to make false teeth	YORVI	False teeth
One of the inventors of a machine for making barbed wire (first name)	BOJCA	Barbed wire
Name of the camera film with a wind-on film	DAKKO	Photography
Moon-based	RLANU	Calendar
Invention that replaced the tinder box	MHTCA	Matches
Marconi shared this prize with another radio pioneer	LBEON	Radio
Tape recorders use plastic tape coated with iron -----	DIXEO	Tape recording
Means of powering a bicycle	LADEP	Bicycle
Used for writing with ink before the invention of the ballpoint pen	LIQLU	Ballpoint pen
Gillette made blades for this	ZORRA	Safety razor
Describes a credit card with a built-in microchip	TASMR	Credit card
Type of mill with sails mounted on top	WROTE	Windmill
Feature of Bramah's improved water closet	NUBDE	Water closet
Dunlop tyres are inflated with air through this	LEAVV	Air-filled tyre
Ancient spindles consisted of a thin stick weighted with this round stone	LWOHR	Spinning
Name of first machine for making one copy of a document at a time	REXXO	Photocopier
Units for measuring distance	DRASY	General
Noughts	RZSOE	General

Index

Picture Acknowledgements

a = above b = below
Barnaby's Picture Library: 56b; 68a; 80a; 91a; 92b; 104b; 106b. Bridgeman Art Library: 9a (Staatliche Antikensammlung, Munich); 14a Louvre); 15b (British Library); 17a (Bibliotheque Nationale); 17b (British Museum); 18b (Staatliche Gemalde-Galerie, Berlin); 23b (Lambeth Palace Library); 25b (British Library); 27a (School of African and Oriental Studies, London); 32a (Science Museum); 32b (Bonhams); 38a (American Museum, Bath); 44b; 45a; 47a (Guildhall Library); 47b; 50a (British Museum). E.T. Archive: 12b; 75a. Format Photographers: 70a (Sharma); 79b (Prince); 93a (Prince); 93b (Prince); 107a (Prince); 107b (Prince). Robert Harding Picture Library: 8a (Kennett); 9b (Wood); 11a (Rainbird); 13a (Wilson); 13b (Sassoon); 16b (Sassoon); 19a (Kennett); 19b (Maxwell); 22a; 22b (Rainbird); 26a (Phillips); 26b (Woolfitt); 29b (Rainbird); 33b (Explorer); 34b; 35b (Rainbird); 40a (Sassoon); 50c (Servian); 52a (Rainbird); 55b (IPC/Ideal Home); 57a (Watts); 58b (Rainbird); 60b (Rainbird); 61b (IPC/Ideal Home); 63b (Rainbird); 67a (Rainbird); 69b (Rawlings); 78a (Richardson); 82a (Griffiths); 82b (Griffiths); 83a (Maxwell); 84b (Harding); 85a; 85b (CA Bild Limhammy Andreasson); 86a (Rainbird); 97a (Evans); 98b (Bildagentur/Schuster Gluster); 100a (Bildagentur /Schuster Bramaz); 100b (Rainbird); 101a (Pottage); 101b(Bildagentur/ Schuster Gerard); 103a (IPC/ Ideal Home); 105a (Victor Watts); 105b. Michael Holford: 10a; 11b; 50b. Hulton-Deutsch Collection: 48a; 48b; 49b; 55a; 64a; 66a; 69a; 74a; 78b; 80b; 89a; 92a; 96a; 98a. Image Bank (Schuster); 70b (Belber); 73b (Schneps); 81a (Lockyer); 96b (Romilly Lockyer); 102a (Elson). Ann Ronan at Image Select: 12a; 14b; 15a; 16a; 18a; 20a; 23a; 24a; 35a; 39a; 39b; 40b; 42b; 45b; 52b; 53a; 53b; 58a; 61a; 62a; 65a; 71b; 72b; 74b; 76b; 106a. Mary Evans Picture Library: 8b; 10b; 20b; 21a; 25a, 27b; 28a; 28b; 29a; 30a; 30b; 31a; 31b; 33a; 34a; 36a; 38b; 41a; 41b; 43a; 43b; 44a; 46a; 46b; 49a; 51b; 57b; 59a; 59b; 60a; 62b; 64b; 67b; 72a; 87b. Philips Consumer Electrics: 103b. Robert Opie Collection: 54a, 54b; 56a; 73a; 79a; 102b. Range Pictures/Bettman: 21b; 81b; 97b; 104a. Martin Breese/Retrograph Archive: 63a; 65b; 66b; 71a; 76a; 86b; 87a; 89b; 90; 94a; 95; 99a; 99b. University of Reading, Rural History Centre: 36b. Science Photo Library: 37a (J. Stevenson); 37b (J. Greim); 77b (C. Priest); 83b (J. Howard); 88a (S. Terry); 88b (S. Stammers).
Front cover:
(clockwise from top left):
Robert Harding Picture Library (Pottage); Bridgeman Art Library; Bridgeman Art Library; Robert Harding (Sassoon); Bridgeman Art Library; Mary Evans Picture Library; Mary Evans Picture Library; Robert Harding (Phillips); Mary Evans Picture Library; Robert Harding Picture Library (Richardson); Robert Harding Picture Library (Lazio /Rainford); Bridgeman Art Library.
Back cover:
(clockwise from top left);
Mary Evans Picture Library; Robert Harding Picture Library (Watts); Robert Harding Picture Library (IPD/Ideal Home); Mary Evans Picture Library; Mary Evans Picture Library; Robert Harding Picture Library (Rainbird); Mary Evans Picture Library; Bridgeman Art Library; Ann Ronan at Image Select; Robert Harding Picture Library (IPC/Ideal Home).
Introduction:
Robert Harding Picture Library (Bildagentur/Schuster Bramaz): 6a (left), Mary Evans Picture Library: 6a (right). Ann Ronan at Image Select: 6b Robert Harding Picture Library (Rawlings): 7a. Bridgeman Art Library (British Library): 7b.
Quiz
(clockwise from top right):
Robert Harding Picture Library (Griffiths); Science Photo Library (J. Stevenson); Barnaby's Picture Library (Bowles); Science Photo Library (S. Stammers); Bridgeman Art Library; Mary Evans Picture Library; Robert Harding Picture Library (Rainbird; Robert Harding Picture Library (Maxwell); Robert Opie Collection